COOKIES & CRUMBS

KAJA HENGSTENBERG

Photography by Lennart Weibull

Hardie Grant

QUADRILLE

saffron, pistachio & white choc cookies, page 94.

STARTING A COOKIE BUSINESS

I'm used to living in different countries and eating and exploring food from different places. I was born in Germany, spent parts of my childhood in Poland, and have enjoyed spells in various cities including London, New York, Berlin and Paris as an adult. I finally ended up in Brussels working as a political consultant, but alongside my job, food was increasingly taking my attention.

The sudden and unexpected death of my father was what made me decide to quit my job and pursue my culinary passion. Not long after that, in August 2019, my Swedish boyfriend and I moved to Stockholm. I was ready to embark on a culinary adventure.

I still remember the first time I ate a soft, American cookie. I was 14 years old and my best friend had brought home a roll of ready-made cookie dough from the USA. I went into raptures over it, and thereafter, each time she or anyone else I knew crossed the Atlantic, I would ask them to buy me a couple of rolls of dough. Recently, while looking at some old photos, I realized that cookies actually cropped up a fair bit. It was my love of cookies combined with a curiosity about different flavour combinations and spices that gave me the idea of opening a cookie shop. What's more, there was nothing like it in Sweden at the time.

I was keen to start my own business and felt that the most important thing was that I did everything my way. Once I get started on something, it's always full speed ahead with me, so I have my friend Sophia to thank for making sure I didn't just take the first retail space I saw. After all, it was the middle of the pandemic so it made more sense to start on a small scale from my kitchen at home. By late 2020, I was engrossed in writing my business plan, testing recipes (some took ages to get just right), thinking about my brand profile, and finding the right ingredients and the right packaging.

As well as building a website and forcing my friends to try out all my new cookies, I also got up to speed on all the rules and regulations around food, and I started doing my own accounts. The walls of my hallway were lined with boxes while my kitchen was full to bursting with stores of flour, chocolate and sugar, which I was fortunately able to receive via my favourite wine bar E&G, since the shipping company wouldn't deliver to residential addresses. Once a week, I packed my big rucksack with 12-kilo bags of flour and 5-kilo packs of butter and lugged it all home from the bar. Finding a good chocolate supplier was tricky, so to begin with I had my favourite French chocolate shipped alternately

7

Mango, coconut & chilli cookies, page 90

Double chocolate & liquorice cookies, page 92

Tomato & vanilla cookies, page 112

Trays of cookies in Kaja's shop on Stockholm's Valhallavägen.

to my mother and sister in Germany and they had the dubious pleasure of forwarding it all on to me in Stockholm.

Then – just like now – all the packaging was done by hand. I folded the brown boxes and lined them with tissue paper while getting through podcast after podcast on food and entrepreneurship. The finishing touch was the blue sticker adorned with the Krümel logo designed for me by a pal in Berlin. My boyfriend Johan was my rock, pitching in not only with the assembly of boxes, but also by

helping me unwind after my intense days –
not to mention putting up with our apartment
being transformed into a warehouse for a
cookie start-up.

Entrepreneurship was new to me, but
I took everything one step at a time and
fortunately most things went well. The feeling I
had on the day when I was able to say 'we're
up and running' was better than anything
else I've ever experienced professionally. I
started by sending cookies to people on the
Stockholm food scene, and their feedback
was both heart-warming and motivational.
Thanks to them and all my hard work on social
media, word spread quickly and in five hours
I had sold out my first two weeks of cookie
deliveries. Naively, I believed I would be
able to do all the deliveries myself on foot
and by bicycle, but I quickly realized that I
needed logistical support from a company that
could help me with my deliveries, not just in
Stockholm but nationwide. Krümel – Cookies
& Crumbs was up and running.

Another thing that helped business take
off was having a signature cookie. In our case,
it was the crumb brûlée – a vanilla-flavoured
cookie filled with cream and topped with
sugar that was caramelized using a blow
torch. It was a massive hit and remains one
of our bestsellers.

The months went by and the wheels
of commerce spun faster and faster. We'd
have businesses ordering up to 500 cookies
for special events, and I did three sold-out
pop-ups together with mates – yet my
equipment consisted of nothing more than
two domestic kitchen appliances that could
only make batter for 50 cookies at a time.
This meant that preparation was always very
time consuming, and before long it was time
to look for a new home.

In the summer of 2021, I began to search for
more suitable premises and six months later
I found what I needed. At the intersection of
Odengatan and Valhallavägen there was a
location that had previously been a bakery.
It wasn't big, but after a quick spruce-up it
was perfect. On 24 April 2021, we (Clara and
I; by then I had taken on my first employee)
opened our doors to the public. We sold out
our 800 cookies before closing time, and I was
so thrilled and grateful – just as I have been
every day since then – about the raptures
our customers went into, and all their positive
feedback. At the beginning, I thought I would
do most of it myself, but now I have a few
employees who help me out with the baking
and sales – we're a really wonderful
cookie team!

I don't know what the future holds for us
– maybe we'll open at more locations or even
branch out into other cities – but for now, I just
want to enjoy what I've created over the last
two years.

New York is probably the place that has given me the most inspiration – and if you like food, then I guarantee that New York is the right city for you too. You can buy an incredible pizza slice on every street corner, there are restaurants, bakeries and patisseries everywhere, and you can try food from any part of the world. Not to mention the plethora of cookie stores. What's more, practically every single café has its own version – most often a chocolate chip cookie – in its range of baked goods.

The first time I visited New York, my focus wasn't on gorging myself on the city's cookies – I was there to do an internship at the UN. I was convinced that I was destined for a career in policymaking, but I found myself constantly and impatiently longing for the weekend and all the food that I would be able to try out when it arrived – Texas barbecue, dumplings, or maybe donuts? I remember the first magical bite of a chocolate vanilla cupcake at Magnolia Bakery: the soft outer crust and the super-creamy buttercream with its intense hit of chocolate. Or their magnificent banana pudding which disappeared in a flash... My taste in baked goods may have changed since then, but I'll never forget those moments.

The second time I visited New York, I had done my research in advance and knew just where to go for bagels the size of my face and where to scoff the best tacos in town while standing in the street, although I did skip the torment of waiting in the crazy long line at Levain Bakery for the best-known cookies in town. Something I didn't miss out on was the famous Milk Bar crack pie and compost cookie, although at the time I had no idea that all these experiences would later inspire me to start my own business.

On my third visit, I had a hitlist. By then, I had started my own cookie shop and I was there to find the best cookies in town and maybe get a little inspiration for new flavour combinations while I was passing through. New York is home to many iconic bakeries famous for their cookies, but if I'm honest I was pretty disappointed with most of the well-known names – too sweet, too artificial, and poor-quality chocolate. Instead, my favourites turned out to be the cookies from small cafés tucked away around the city, often still family-owned, like Librae, Red Gate Bakery and Supermoon Bakehouse.

The first new cookie I created after I came home was the NYC crumb, flavoured with pumpkin spice, rolled in roasted pecans and topped with maple syrup. It's an homage to an irresistible donut I ate at Pies n' Thighs in Williamsburg. It was an instant hit and I'll most definitely be drawing upon the City of New York for inspiration for more cookies in future.

EQUIPMENT

You don't need any special equipment to bake cookies. A kitchen stand mixer comes in handy, but it isn't a necessity. I do recommend, however, that you get an electric whisk, since it can be difficult to mix sugar and butter by hand. You probably already have everything else you need in your kitchen.

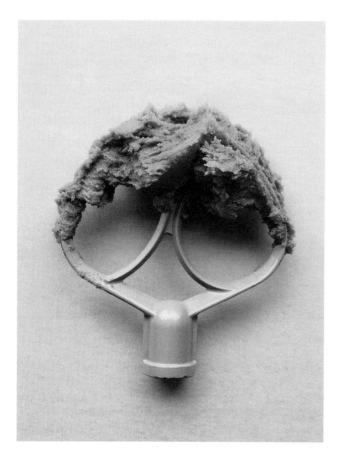

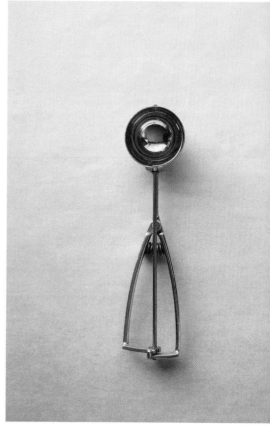

Baking parchment/silicone mat
In the shop, we only ever use baking parchment, but when I was baking at home I also used silicone mats. Both methods work, but I noticed that some cookies baked on silicone expanded a little too much and got taller during the bake than I wanted them to.

Baking trays
I use regular 30 x 40cm (12 x 16in) baking trays – I prefer to use ones with low edges since this ensures better air circulation.

Balloon whisk
Ideal for mixing flour, baking powder and bicarbonate of soda (baking soda). And melted butter with sugar and eggs.

Bowls
I usually weigh out all the different ingredients into bowls beforehand to make my baking more organized.

Cookie cutter
Your cookies will be completely delicious even if they are a little uneven and have spread out, but a cookie cutter is handy if you want to ensure they're perfectly circular. I always have a 7–8cm (3in) cookie cutter on hand to round off cookies after baking. You can use the off-cuts in the recipes for leftover cookies at the end of the book.

Cookie dough scoop

I use the kind of ice cream scoop that helps to nudge the ball of ice cream out of the scoop. Mine is 56mm (2in) in diameter and gives you a dough ball weighing 65g (2¼oz) – perfect for every cookie recipe. If you don't have a scoop like that, then it's fine to use a regular tablespoon

Grater

I use a Microplane grater when zesting fruit. It is a precise tool and works well even for fruit with thin skin, such as tangerines. Any regular fine grater will also be suitable.

Kitchen blow torch

A kitchen blow torch is only needed for two recipes in this book (the ube brûlée and the s'mores cookie), but it's well worth getting one – especially if you like making regular crème brûlées. My recommendation is not to go for the very cheapest model, but choose a mid-priced blow torch instead, which should ensure far better results.

Oven

I prefer baking cookies in a fan oven since this guarantees the best results. Air circulates from all sides, ensuring the cookies are evenly baked while remaining gooey inside and having slightly crunchy surfaces and edges. A regular oven with just top and bottom heat is also fine, but you may need to adjust your baking times. If using a fan oven, you need a slightly lower temperature than a regular oven (follow the directions in the recipes).

Ube brûlée cookies, page 98

Spatula

I use a spatula with a metal handle and rubber head for all my recipes. It needs to offer a little flexibility but should be fairly rigid, making it perfect for scraping mixture from the dough bowl.

Stand mixer

I *love* my stand mixer. They're pretty pricey, but last for a long time. I've had mine for nine years and to date it's caused me no trouble. The advantage is that you can use both of your hands to add ingredients while the mixer is running, and you can opt for different speed settings. With a hand-held electric whisk or hand-held blender, you have to keep stopping and switching off the appliance in order to add new ingredients. But this is mostly a practical consideration – if all you have is an electric whisk then that's fine. Your cookies will be just as tasty! Apart from the recipes you should mix by hand, and one of the gluten-free recipes, I always use the paddle attachment (see page 18).

Scales

I always weigh my ingredients instead of using volume measures. This ensures better precision in terms of both measurements and outcomes, and once you've started using scales you won't regret it. Entry-level scales can't generally be used for particularly light weights (1–5g/less than ⅛ oz), which is why I have also included volumes in teaspoons and tablespoons in the recipes.

INGREDIENTS & TECHNIQUES

I want to teach you everything I can about baking cookies. I've always known in my head how my cookies should taste, but finding the right flavours and textures in practice has taken persistence and has at times been pretty frustrating. Some recipes work right off the bat while others have taken hours and a ton of flour and butter before they've been right. I've baked cookies that have melted into a gooey mess, some have never progressed beyond a rock-solid lump, and others have looked perfect on the tray but been completely raw inside.

Here are my top tips and hints to make sure you avoid frustration on the way to your perfect cookies. If you follow my advice, follow the recipes and use good ingredients, then there's not much that can go wrong.

Prep is everything

Before we go through the specific ingredients, I want to
emphasize the importance of preparing in advance. Take
out and weigh all your ingredients before you start mixing
the dough.

I put the following into separate bowls: butter, sugar,
other dry ingredients, and chocolate. I keep my eggs
out on the side. It's better to realize that you're missing
something at this stage than to have to nip round to the
neighbours to borrow something once you've actually
started work.

Another plus point of doing it this way is that all the
ingredients are at the same temperature, which means
the dough combines better. Everything should be at room
temperature (or at least in the range of 16–20°C/
60–70°F) unless otherwise stated in the recipe. There's
no need to measure this – just make sure you take your
chilled ingredients out of the refrigerator about 20 minutes
before you start mixing your dough.

INGREDIENTS

If you want to make really tasty cookies, then you should use the best ingredients you can. Meh flour makes meh cookies, and the same is true for poor-quality chocolate, eggs and butter. But, if all you have in is long-term cupboard ingredients (or you don't want to change out of your pyjamas to go to the shops), then it's still more fun to bake than not to bake at all. You'll end up with cookies at any rate.

Baking powder & bicarbonate of soda (baking soda)

Most of my recipes contain both baking powder and bicarbonate of soda (baking soda). Bicarbonate neutralizes the acidity in the cookies and makes them expand a little, while the baking powder gives them a real boost to ensure they rise nicely in the oven.

Baking powder consists of bicarbonate of soda, an acid such as cream of tartar, and a binding agent such as cornflour (cornstarch). When added to a dough, it reacts twice: first when it comes into contact with the moisture in the dough, and again when it comes into contact with the warmth of the oven. Baking powder ensures that your cookies rise and also expand a little. However, bicarbonate of soda only reacts with acidic ingredients like dark chocolate.

Butter

Butter is an important ingredient in cookies, not only for its flavour but also its texture. In Sweden, retail butter usually has a fat content of 80–82 per cent. I always choose the highest possible fat content I can find since this ensures a softer crust and better consistency. Fat also means flavour. The more fat there is, the less water the butter contains. When mixing butter with sugar, it's the water in the butter that dissolves the sugar crystals. When you bake cookies, the water evaporates which gives a crispier crust and cakier texture.

On the other hand, if you melt or brown the butter, then most of the water in the butter evaporates before you add the other ingredients. This means you don't aerate the dough, which results in heavier, tougher cookies. I'll go into more detail about that in the techniques section.

I've always baked with salted butter, but I recommend that you use unsalted. In recent years, I've used exactly the same product so I know how much salt I need to add to my dough, but since the quantity of salt can vary so much between different producers (French salted butter is far saltier than its Swedish equivalent, for example) it's easier to use unsalted.

Three types of chocolate pellets: white, dark and milk.

Chocolate

You want the best possible chocolate in your cookies. The French brand Valrhona, and Callebaut from Belgium are my two favourites. Jivara is an incredible milk chocolate, while Tropilia Amer is an excellent dark chocolate with a dash of bitterness to it. My preferred brand when making vegan cookies is always Malmö Chokladfabrik. I never use baking chocolate, since it often contains added oils and other additives that I don't like.

Cocoa

I always use dark cocoa from Valrhona in my cookies – there's no added sugar or any other additives. It has a slightly earthy taste and an intense flavour that is perfect for baking with. It's also known as Dutch process cocoa powder since it goes through an alkalizing process that softens the taste, gives it a darker colour and neutralizes the acid from the cocoa. If you prefer a cheaper alternative or can't find Valrhona, there are plenty of other brands to choose from. Check out the baking section in your local supermarket.

Eggs

Eggs add moisture and fat to your cookies. Additionally, they provide structure, some flavour and colour (if you've ever baked with a really orange egg, you'll probably have noticed this already!). The recipes in this book are based on medium-sized eggs weighing about 64g (2¼oz) each. Buy the best eggs you can find.

Flour

I always use organic flour. It contains a lot of minerals, is unprocessed and unbleached. I never use self-raising flour since I prefer to remain in control of the quantity of baking powder that gets added. If you use flour from a small mill, the character may vary from batch to batch. I only use flour from a small mill on the Swedish west coast that offers all the varieties I need. The base is usually wheat flour (except when baking gluten-free cookies) and then I add a proportion of heritage grains such as spelt, emmer or rye to add extra depth, nuttiness, sweetness and earthiness.

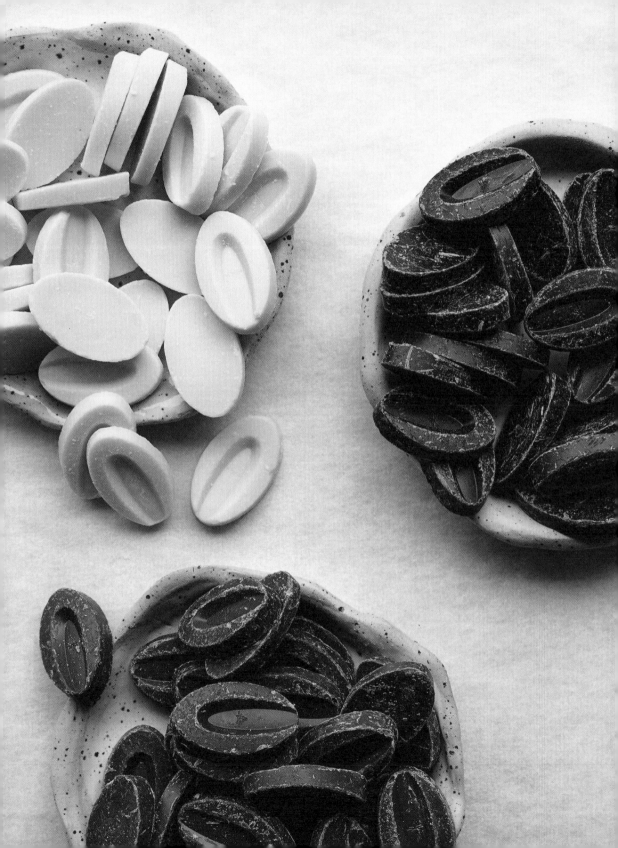

Pay attention to the best before label on your flour. It's often fine to bake with even if it's past its best, but if it's too old then it may have lost its good flavour or even acquired an unwanted aftertaste.

Freeze-dried fruit

As the name suggests, freeze-dried fruit is fruit dried using a special process that preserves more of the flavour profile than other methods. This makes them great for baking with. I like to add freeze-dried fruit in powdered form to my bakes in order to boost the flavour without changing the texture of the cookie. You can buy freeze-dried fruit from specialist stores or online. Store them in airtight containers so that they don't absorb moisture from the air around them.

Nuts

Always toast nuts before using them, as this releases their oils and flavour. I usually chop them roughly, but it's up to you what you do – you can always use them whole.

Salt

I use fine salt in my dough and Maldon sea salt flakes or French sea salt to top my cookies after baking. It's fine to use those kinds of salt flakes in your dough too, but you often need a little extra since the taste is usually more subtle.

Sugar

My mother always tried to ensure that my sister and I ate as little sugar as possible in the form of confectionery, and she often used honey instead of sugar in desserts.

However, she was always on team sugar when it came to baking. If you try to replace the sugar with something else, the result often ends up differing from what you expected. I'm not a fan of artificial sweeteners or overly saccharine flavours, and when I say I'm using sugar in a recipe, that's what I use. What's important is finding the right balance of sweetness.

In my recipes, I always use a mix of white and brown sugar. They have different qualities, which means the ratio will vary. If you want crispy edges and a nice crispy surface, then nothing beats white sugar in your dough.

BROWN SUGAR

My brown sugar of choice is light muscovado sugar. It's a little more expensive but it makes a big difference. Brown sugar contains lots of molasses and moisture, and it has a far deeper flavour profile than white sugar. Brown sugar results in a heavier cookie that expands more. The denser structure doesn't combine with butter in quite the same way as white sugar when you beat it, which means it retains less air. The outcome is a less fluffy cookie that also comes out darker and with a softer surface.

WHITE SUGAR

It's easy to get hold of caster sugar in the UK and a finer grain of granulated sugar in the USA. But it's harder to get hold of fine-grained white sugar in Sweden, so my recipes have been written with regular Swedish granulated sugar in mind. White sugar gives the cookies a lighter colour and means they don't expand as much. The texture is also airier and cakier, while retaining a crispier touch on the surface and edges.

Syrup

In a handful of recipes I use syrup to make my cookies lighter and less moist. When I do, I always use dark sugar beet syrup.

Vanilla

In these recipes I use vanilla powder. It is made by drying vanilla pods and grinding them into a fine powder. This is less powerful than a fresh vanilla pod, but it is easier to add to your dough.

If you have vanilla pods then feel free to use them in the recipes instead of powder. Personally, I prefer to keep them for desserts where the vanilla taste plays a more central role than it does in cookies. The vanilla flavour varies depending on where it was grown. Mexican vanilla is usually spicy, while Madagascan vanilla features that classic sweet and creamy flavour.

You can use vanilla extract if you like, but I think it's akin to alcohol in that it's a little sharp in tone, and I'm not very fond of that.

TECHNIQUES

There are probably almost as many cookie recipes as there are people on the planet.

With so many different recipes out there, it goes without saying that there is also a plethora of views on mixing times and methods. I've geeked out on all of this – so to save you the trouble, here are my top tips.

Rule number one: follow the recipes. I like to freestyle in the kitchen, but it's never a good idea when you're baking – doing so will only leave you unnecessarily frustrated. It's easier to experiment with flavouring, but if you do so, make sure you're strict when it comes to butter, sugar and flour.

Mixing the butter and sugar for too long

In order to make a soft and gooey cookie, you have to beat the butter and sugar enough – but not too much. There's a fine line between mixing too much and mixing too little. I've concluded that I get the best results when I whisk the two ingredients for 1½–2 minutes. The mixture should become a little lighter, but it shouldn't be pale and super fluffy.

You beat the sugar and butter to add air bubbles and to dissolve the sugar crystals and distribute them evenly in the batter. The air bubbles in the dough puff up in the high temperatures inside the oven and are effectively no different to baking powder and bicarbonate of soda (baking soda) in that they act as a rising agent.

If you beat the sugar and butter for longer than 1½–2 minutes then the consistency ends up very light and fluffy, which means that the final cookie ends up very cakey. If you continue to beat the ingredients for 4–5 minutes then the risk is that the cookies will rise even more before collapsing when you take them out of the oven since the structure of the dough will be unable to retain all the air.

Not beating the butter and sugar for long enough

If you don't beat the butter and sugar for long enough, then the batter ends up dense and is often much too sticky. Since the batter hasn't been combined properly, it doesn't act as a raising agent. The butter melts, the cookie expands and you can feel the sugar crystals when eating it.

Beating the eggs for too long

If you beat the eggs in the batter for so long that the batter ends up completely smooth and creamy, then you've been whisking for too long. That's certainly the case if you're baking chunky and gooey or soft and gooey cookies.

You want it to be a little unevenly mixed with some traces of the egg still visible. It's different in the case of chewy cookies where you're whisking by hand and a more even batter is preferable.

Butter

Cookies can be divided into three main categories in terms of consistency. The different categories require butter in different forms: cold, room temperature or melted.

COLD BUTTER

Cold means that the butter should be at refrigerator temperature. If it is supposed to be diced, make sure you do this at the beginning of your preparations and return the diced butter to the refrigerator. Don't take it out until it's time to add it to your mixture.

SOFT/ROOM TEMPERATURE BUTTER

Butter at this temperature is supposed to be pliable but not super soft. If you press your fingertips into it, there should still be some resistance.

MELTED BUTTER

Melt the butter slowly over a low heat. When it melts, some water evaporates, so you'll need slightly more melted butter if you're replacing soft butter with melted. Once the butter has melted, leave it to cool to room temperature – this should take 20–30 minutes.

BROWN BUTTER

There are two recipes in the book that use brown butter. This is really just melted butter taken a bit further so even more water has evaporated from it. The brown butter takes on a wonderful, nutty, caramelized tone.

Mixing in the flour for too long

When adding flour, you should never mix it in for longer than necessary; just ensure that the flour combines into the batter and that it is no longer lumpy. If you keep mixing for longer, this will result in the formation of gluten networks that make the cookies too dense. Add a little flour at a time and scrape down the sides of the bowl as you go. If you don't spend long enough mixing in the flour, you'll end up with pockets of flour in your cookies.

Scrape everything down from the edges

Make sure that all the butter, sugar, eggs and flour are scraped down from the inside of the bowl – otherwise there's a risk that your dough will contain lumps of butter and pockets of flour, and your cookies will end up in weird shapes during the bake.

Leave the dough to cool

Always put your dough or dough balls (depending on the recipe) into the refrigerator. A chilled dough gives your cookies better structure since the butter doesn't melt as quickly in the oven. If it melts too quickly, then the cookies end up flatter. The taste is also improved if your dough has been left to cool since it gives the flour time to hydrate while the other flavours develop, helping to ensure it becomes a more intense whole. If you can, I recommend leaving your cookie dough in the refrigerator for 24 hours, but you should always ensure it rests for a minimum of 3 hours. Always cover your bowl with a lid or wrap the dough with cling film (plastic wrap) so that it doesn't dry out.

Baking

Always preheat the oven so that it has reached a stable temperature. If you put your cookies into an oven that is too cold, the bake will take longer and your cookies will end up dry and flat. I always preheat my oven at home for 20 minutes.

I use the oven in fan oven mode. I've tested baking cookies with and without the fan and concluded that the fan ensures a more even bake, while the cookies don't take on too much colour and remain soft on the inside. The fan also allows you to have two trays in the oven at the same time. If you don't have a fan oven then it's obviously fine to bake without, but you should stick to one tray at a time. Place the tray in the middle of the oven so that it benefits from both the top and bottom heat. Be careful not to put too many cookies on each tray. Too many cookies in the oven at once makes the humidity in the oven too high and extends your baking time.

Too much steam means that the cookies are unable to form the thin, crunchy surface we're after. There's also the risk that they will end up merging on the tray. The number of trays that you can bake at the same time varies from oven to oven – mine can manage two but not three.

Don't open the oven door unnecessarily

Having a tray of cookies in the oven feels like Christmas morning, but try to resist the temptation to open the door to take a look or get a whiff of that lovely smell. Heat escapes each time the door opens and it can cause the air to escape from your cookies too. Instead, settle down with a book for the 9–12 minutes you have to wait.

When are my cookies baked?

The cookies are ready when they have expanded. They should be golden in colour, their edges should be a little darker and the top should have a slight sheen but should be mostly dry. The surface should not have cracked – if it has, the cookies have been in the oven too long and will be dry. Don't forget that they keep on cooking after being removed from the oven as they set and the inside becomes a little less gooey. Make sure you leave them to stand for a few minutes before eating them. I've also noticed that they taste much sweeter before they have cooled properly.

How long do cookies keep for?

Cookies are obviously tastiest when eaten on the day they are baked, but they should remain delicious for 3–5 days. Don't put them in the microwave (they end up too soft) and don't keep them in the refrigerator (they end up too dry). You can freeze cooled down, fully baked cookies, or your prepared cookie dough. You can defrost a baked cookie and then warm it up for 2–3 minutes at 160°C fan (180°C/350°F/gas 4). A frozen cookie can also be warmed up in the oven from frozen; this takes around 5–7 minutes.

Freezing dough balls is a perfect way to ensure you always have cookies on hand. To cook a frozen dough ball, just add 2 minutes to the baking time in the recipe.

A note on my recipes

Most of the recipes in this book are written assuming that you'll use a food processor or stand mixer with more speeds than an electric whisk. When I use a stand mixer, I mix the flour and dry ingredients into the butter in two steps. When I use an electric whisk/hand-held blender, I instead fold in the flour using a wooden spatula – and I do the same with dried fruit and chocolate. This ensures that the dough doesn't get over-worked since you only want it to just come together.

Too hard/dry – too much flour or white sugar or too long in the oven? Check the oven temperature!

Too crunchy – too much flour or too little moisture? Maybe too long in the oven?

HAS SOMETHING GONE AWRY?

Everything should go fine if you follow the recipes, but sometimes you miss something or take a shortcut. Here are a few troubleshooting points to figure out what may have gone awry with your cookies.

Too cakey – too many eggs (were your eggs unusually large?) or too much baking powder? Too much white sugar? Maybe you beat the sugar and butter for too long?

Too yellow – this is nothing to worry about; maybe you just used eggs with unusually yellow yolks? Or perhaps you added too much bicarbonate of soda (baking soda)?

Too dense (in a bad way) – maybe you mixed the flour for too long? Did you beat the butter for too long, or perhaps not enough?

Not expanding enough – too much flour or too little butter? Too much white sugar and not enough brown sugar? Was the oven too hot?

Expands too much – maybe you didn't leave the dough in the refrigerator for long enough? Was the butter too soft when it was beaten? Too little flour? Was the oven hot enough?

Too flat – maybe you didn't leave the dough in the refrigerator for long enough? Maybe you beat the eggs and sugar for too long, or perhaps not for long enough? Was the oven hot enough?

Too crispy – maybe you didn't leave the dough in the refrigerator for long enough? Too much white sugar? Too long in the oven?

Too small/didn't rise in the oven – check that your baking powder isn't out of date. Maybe you left your dough to rest in the refrigerator for more than a few days, meaning that the baking powder became less effective?

GOOEY & CHUNKY

Banana & walnut cookies
as dough balls and fully
baked cookies.

Gooey & chunky is a category of cookie that is a little heavier than the other two varieties in this book. These cookies are very soft and gooey on the inside, and almost seem as if they haven't been baked through. They bake in the oven at 190°C fan (210°C/410°F/gas 6–7), which means they end up darker, have a crunchier surface and are thicker in the centre with thinner edges. They're chunky because they're filled with chocolate, dried fruit or nuts, and they also weigh more than the other types of cookies in this book.

When baking soft and gooey cookies, cold butter is your worst enemy, but in chunky cookies this is exactly what you want. Cold, diced butter should be added to your mixture straight from the refrigerator, and you also have to make sure that you cool your dough balls before baking them. This ensures your cookies rise properly and come out nice and chunky.

The first step is always to beat the butter just to break it up a little. Then you add and partly mix in the sugar, but not so much that it ends up as a homogeneous batter – you want to leave a few small lumps of butter. The eggs should then be added and whisked quickly, but make sure they don't end up fully incorporated into the batter either. After that you add the flour over two stages before you finally add any nuts or dried fruit. The process might be reminiscent of how you make shortbread or scones, but we're not aiming for crispness – what we want is a really gooey centre, a good height and a crunchy outer layer.

Dough

The dough will feel denser, cooler and less pliable than it does when making soft and gooey dough. Aim to make dough balls that weigh around 75g (2½oz) each, but avoid rolling them so that they don't end up completely smooth – it's better if they're a little irregular in shape. You can accomplish this by pressing them into an approximate ball shape after weighing them. Place them in a plastic container and leave to cool in the refrigerator for at least 3 hours before baking.

Baking

Chunky cookies are baked at a high temperature for a shorter time. They also don't expand as much, which makes them thicker and gives them a darker, crunchier surface.

Texture

Inside they should be gooey and almost underbaked, but if you've followed the recipe, then they'll be just as they should be.

MILK CHOCOLATE CHIP COOKIES

190g (6¾oz/¾ cup plus 1⅓ Tbsp) butter at refrigerator temperature, diced

150g (5½oz/¾ cup) light muscovado sugar

100g (3½oz/½ cup) caster (granulated) sugar

2 eggs

350g (12oz/2⅔ cups) plain (all-purpose) flour

15g (½oz/1 Tbsp) cornflour (cornstarch)

5g (1⅔ tsp) baking powder

3g (1 tsp) salt

200g (7oz) milk chocolate, roughly chopped

ABOUT 15 COOKIES

This is a recipe for a classic chunky cookie. While it may be a classic chocolate chip cookie, it tastes and looks different from ones made using brown butter. The dough needs to be ever-so-slightly denser and a little coarser and more uneven, while it bakes for a little less time but at a higher temperature. All this makes for a pretty tall cookie with a crunchy outer crust and a wonderfully gooey centre. Chocolate is the most important ingredient in this recipe, so make sure that yours is good quality: I find that Valrhona Jivara is the perfect addition to this recipe.

Add the butter to your food processor or to the bowl of a stand mixer fitted with a paddle attachment and mix on a medium speed for 15 seconds until the butter begins to break up. Add both types of sugar and mix for about 30 seconds until everything is roughly mixed. Scrape the butter from the sides of the bowl.

Add the eggs and mix for 20 seconds until everything is just combined. Make sure you don't mix for too long – it's fine if it's still a little unmixed.

Combine the flour, cornflour, baking powder and salt in a separate bowl. Add the dry ingredients to the butter mixture in two batches, mixing for 15 seconds between each batch until everything is just combined. Scrape the base and sides of the bowl between each round of mixing.

Finally, add the chocolate and mix at a low speed until the chocolate is roughly mixed into the dough.

Scoop 70g (2½oz) balls of dough using an ice cream scoop, or roll balls using 3 tablespoons of dough. There should be enough to make about 15 cookies. Place the dough balls in a container with a lid or on a tray that you then cover with cling film (plastic wrap). Leave to rest in the refrigerator for at least 3 hours – preferably overnight.

Preheat the oven to 190°C fan (210°C/ 410°F/gas 6–7).

Place the dough balls approximately 5cm (2in) apart on baking trays lined with baking parchment. Bake in the middle of the oven for 9–10 minutes. Bake one sheet at a time if not using a fan oven. The cookies should have expanded a bit, risen and begun to firm, but should still glisten a little bit and should not have cracked.

Remove the trays of cookies from the oven. Leave to cool for 5 minutes, then transfer them to a cooling rack and leave to cool for at least another 10–15 minutes.

BISCOFF & CHOCOLATE COOKIES

190g (6¾oz/¾ cup plus 1⅓ Tbsp) butter at refrigerator temperature, diced

150g (5½oz/¾ cup) light muscovado sugar

100g (3½oz/½ cup) caster (granulated) sugar

2 eggs

350g (12oz/2⅔ cups) plain (all-purpose) flour

15g (½oz/1 Tbsp) cornflour (cornstarch)

5g (1⅔ tsp) baking powder

3g (1 tsp) salt

150g (5½oz) dark chocolate, roughly chopped

10 Lotus Biscoff biscuits/cookies (or use gingerbread biscuits), roughly crumbled

1 jar Lotus Biscoff spread

ABOUT 15 COOKIES

This cookie is a tribute to a treat that was a favourite of mine when I lived in Brussels. It features a Belgian caramelized biscuit base and filling – you know those rectangular, thin, dark brown biscuits you get wrapped in transparent film emblazoned with a red logo? Lotus biscuits! You often get them with your cup of coffee if you're in a café – especially when out and about in Belgium. It so happens that they also make a Biscoff spread which has a peanut butter consistency. You can bake this recipe using those kinds of biscuits and the spread, or you can Swedish-up your version using traditional gingerbread. If you can't find the right spread at the shops, the recipe also works fine with any nut butter of your choosing.

Add the butter to your food processor or to the bowl of a stand mixer fitted with a paddle attachment and mix on a medium speed for 15 seconds until the butter begins to break up. Add both types of sugar and mix for about 30 seconds until everything is roughly mixed. Scrape the butter from the sides of the bowl.

Add the eggs and mix for a maximum of 20 seconds until they are just combined. Make sure you don't mix for too long – it's fine if it's still a little unmixed.

Combine the flour, cornflour, baking powder and salt in a separate bowl. Add the dry ingredients to the butter mixture in two batches, mixing for a maximum of 10–15 seconds between each batch until everything is just combined. Scrape down the base and sides of the bowl between each round of mixing.

Add the chocolate and Biscoff biscuit pieces before mixing at a low speed until the chocolate and biscuits are roughly mixed into the dough.

Scoop 75g (2½oz) balls of dough using an ice cream scoop, or roll balls using 3 tablespoons of dough. There should be enough to make about 15 cookies. Press your thumb into each one to make a deep impression. Add 2 teaspoons of Biscoff spread into each impression and cover with dough before rolling back into a ball to ensure that each ball of cookie dough has a filling. Place the dough balls in a container with a lid or on a tray that you then cover with cling film (plastic wrap). Leave to rest in the refrigerator for at least 3 hours – preferably overnight.

Preheat the oven to 190°C fan (210°C/ 410°F/gas 6–7).

Place the dough balls approximately 5cm (2in) apart on baking trays lined with baking parchment. Bake in the middle of the oven for 9–10 minutes. The cookies should have expanded a bit, risen and begun to firm, but should still glisten a little bit and should not have cracked.

Remove the trays of cookies from the oven and leave to cool for 5 minutes. Transfer them to a cooling rack and leave to cool for at least another 10–15 minutes.

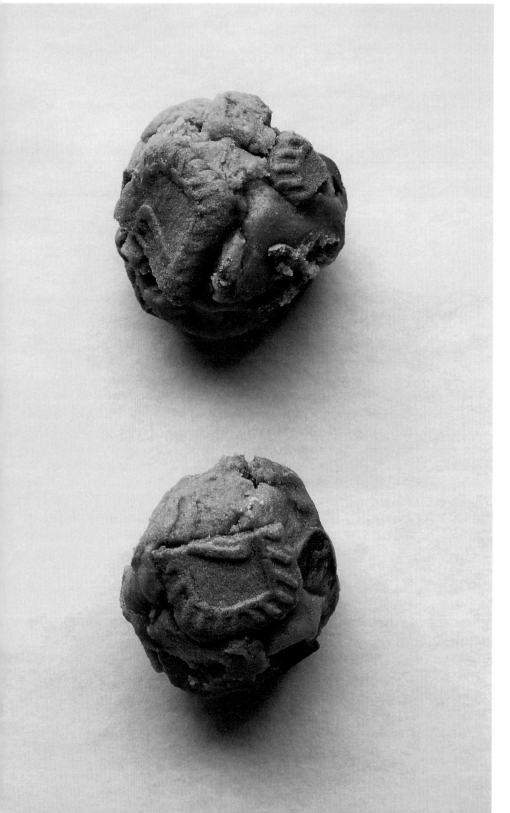

The filling means this cookie is gooey in the middle.

BANANA & WALNUT COOKIES

190g (6¾oz/¾ cup plus 1⅓ Tbsp) butter at
refrigerator temperature, diced

130g (4½oz/⅔ cup) light muscovado sugar

95g (3½oz/½ cup) caster (granulated) sugar

1 very ripe banana

1 egg

310g (11oz/2¼ cups) plain (all-purpose) flour

50g (1¾oz/6 Tbsp) finely ground rye flour

2 tsp lapsang souchong tea leaves, crumbled
(optional)

5g (1⅔ tsp) baking powder

3g (1 tsp) salt

100g (3½oz) milk chocolate, roughly chopped

150g (5½oz) walnuts, roasted and roughly
chopped

ABOUT 15 COOKIES

I love a good banana bread! It has to be dense and full of goodies like chocolate and nuts. I also love a smoky touch to my food... In fact, I once almost moved to Austin, Texas just so that I could eat barbecue sauce. (I'm not kidding!) Of course, you can smoke the bananas, but I wanted to create a recipe that anyone can make at home, which is why I went for a good pinch of lapsang souchong instead – all you have to do is crumble the tea leaves between your fingers. Smoked tea originally comes from China, but nowadays you'll find it in most tea shops. It adds a delicate, earthy and smoky flavour to these delicious banana cookies and makes them something truly special! If you don't like smoky flavours, you can simply skip the tea when making the recipe.

Add the butter to your food processor or to the bowl of a stand mixer fitted with a paddle attachment and mix on a medium speed for 15 seconds until the butter begins to break up. Add both types of sugar. Mix for about 30 seconds until everything is roughly mixed. Scrape the butter from the sides of the bowl. Mash and mix in the banana.

Add the egg and mix for 20 seconds until it is nicely and evenly combined. Make sure you don't mix for too long – it's fine if it's still a little unmixed.

Combine the plain flour, rye flour, tea leaves (if using), baking powder and salt in a separate bowl. Add the dry ingredients to the butter mixture in two batches, mixing for 15 seconds between each batch until everything is just combined. Scrape down the base and sides of the bowl between each round of mixing.

Finally, add the chocolate and walnuts and mix at a low speed until the chocolate is distributed throughout the dough.

Scoop 75g (2½oz) balls of dough using an ice cream scoop, or roll balls using 3 tablespoons of dough. There should be enough to make about 15 cookies. Place the dough balls in a container with a lid or on a tray that you then cover with cling film (plastic wrap). Leave to rest in the refrigerator for at least 3 hours – preferably overnight.

Preheat the oven to 190°C fan (210°C/410°F/gas 6-7).

Place the dough balls approximately 5cm (2in) apart on baking trays lined with baking parchment. Bake in the middle of the oven for 9–10 minutes. The cookies should have expanded a bit, risen and begun to firm, but should still glisten a little bit and should not have cracked.

Remove the trays of cookies from the oven. Leave to cool for 5 minutes, then transfer them to a cooling rack and leave to cool for at least another 10–15 minutes.

OAT COOKIES WITH APRICOT & PISTACHIO DUKKAH

My top tip!

Immediately after mixing, the dough will be pretty wet, but the oats will soak up some of that liquid – that's why it's so important to let the dough rest a while before baking.

230g (8oz/1 cup) butter at refrigerator
temperature, diced

210g (7½oz/1 cup plus 1 Tbsp) light muscovado
sugar

70g (2½oz/5⅔ Tbsp) caster (granulated) sugar

3g (1 tsp) vanilla powder or 2 tsp vanilla extract

2 eggs

350g (12oz/2⅔ cups) plain (all-purpose) flour

30g (1oz/¼ cup) cornflour (cornstarch)

140g (5oz/1½ cups) rolled oats

3g (1½ tsp) ras el hanout

3g (1 tsp) bicarbonate of soda (baking soda)

5g (1⅔ tsp) baking powder

1½g (½ tsp) salt

140g (5oz) dried apricots, roughly chopped

130g (4½oz) roasted pistachios

ABOUT 20 COOKIES

For me, the oat cookie is the proto-cookie of them all and it goes without saying that it has to feature in this book. This is a chunky cookie with an uneven texture and crispy surface, and is super gooey inside. Ras el hanout is a North African spice mix containing cinnamon, nutmeg and cumin, and it is commonly used in cookery. I added it because it has a distinctive nutty taste. Together with the apricot, pistachio and sweet dukkah, it's the perfect combination of sweet, sour, piquant and full-bodied. Like a warm hug!

DUKKAH

3 Tbsp toasted white sesame seeds

50g (1¾oz) roasted pistachios, finely chopped

1 tsp ras el hanout

½ tsp ground cardamom

¼ tsp ground cinnamon

75g (2½oz/6 Tbsp) caster (granulated) sugar

½ tsp sea salt flakes

Combine all the dukkah ingredients in a bowl.

Add the butter to your food processor or to the bowl of a stand mixer fitted with a paddle attachment and mix on a medium speed for 15 seconds until the butter begins to break up. Add the sugars and the vanilla, then mix until the sugar has roughly combined with the butter. Scrape the butter from the sides of the bowl.

Add the eggs and mix for a maximum of 20 seconds until they are just combined. Make sure you don't mix for too long.

Combine the flours, oats, ras el hanout, bicarbonate of soda, baking powder and salt in a separate bowl. Add the dry ingredients to the butter mixture in two batches, mixing for 10–15 seconds between each batch until everything is just combined. Scrape down the base and sides of the bowl between each round of mixing.

Add the apricots and pistachios. Mix at a low speed until they are all roughly combined.

Scoop 75g (2½oz) rough balls of dough using an ice cream scoop, or roll balls using 3 tablespoons of dough. This should be enough for about 20 cookies. Dip one side of each cookie in the dukkah. Place the dough balls in a container with a lid or on a tray that you then cover with cling film (plastic wrap). Leave to rest in the refrigerator for at least 3 hours – preferably overnight.

Preheat the oven to 190°C fan (210°C/ 410°F/gas 6–7).

Place the dough balls, dukkah-side up, approximately 5cm (2in) apart on baking trays lined with baking parchment. Bake in the middle of the oven for 9–10 minutes. Bake one sheet at a time if not using a fan oven. The cookies should have expanded a bit, risen and begun to firm, but should not have cracked.

Transfer them to a cooling rack and leave to cool for at least another 10–15 minutes.

Prune and five-spice oat cookies, page 62.

PRUNE & FIVE-SPICE OAT COOKIES

240g (8½oz/1 cup plus 1 Tbsp) butter at
refrigerator temperature, diced

215g (7½oz/1 cup plus 1 Tbsp) light muscovado sugar

80g (2¾oz/⅓ cup plus 1 Tbsp) caster (granulated) sugar

2 eggs

350g (12oz/2⅔ cups) plain (all-purpose) flour

30g (1oz/¼ cup) cornflour (cornstarch)

140g (5oz/1½ cups) rolled oats

4g (1½ tsp) Chinese five-spice powder

5g (1⅔ tsp) baking powder

2g (⅔ tsp) bicarbonate of soda (baking soda)

1½g (½ tsp) salt

160g (5¾oz) prunes, roughly chopped

ABOUT 18 COOKIES

Prunes and Chinese five-spice are examples of flavours and spices that also work well when baking sweet treats. That's no surprise, given that the mixture consists of spices such as cinnamon, star anise and cloves – particularly welcome in winter. In Poland, there is a common Christmas drink available in the festive season that this cookie is reminiscent of.

SUGAR TOPPING

30g (1oz/2½ Tbsp) caster sugar

1 tsp Chinese five-spice powder

Prepare the topping by mixing the sugar and five-spice in a small bowl. Set aside.

Add the butter to your food processor or to the bowl of a stand mixer fitted with a paddle attachment and mix on a medium speed for 15 seconds until the butter begins to break up. Add both types of sugar and mix for about 30 seconds until everything is roughly mixed. Scrape the butter from the sides of the bowl.

Add the eggs and mix for 20 seconds until everything is just combined. Make sure you don't mix for too long – it's fine if it's still a little unmixed.

Combine the flour, cornflour, rolled oats, five-spice, baking powder, bicarbonate of soda and salt in a separate bowl. Add the dry ingredients to the butter mixture in two batches, mixing for 15–20 seconds between each batch until everything is just combined. Scrape down the base and sides of the bowl between each round of mixing.

Finally, add the prunes and mix at a low speed until they are combined into the dough.

Scoop 75g (2½oz) balls of dough using an ice cream scoop, or roll balls using 3 tablespoons of dough. There should be enough to make about 18 cookies. Roll the balls in the prepared sugar topping mixture. Place the dough balls in a container with a lid or on a tray that you then cover with cling film (plastic wrap). Leave to rest in the refrigerator for at least 3 hours – preferably overnight.

Preheat the oven to 190°C fan (210°C/ 410°F/gas 6–7).

Place the dough balls approximately 5cm (2in) apart on baking trays lined with baking parchment. Bake in the middle of the oven for 9–10 minutes. Bake one sheet at a time if not using a fan oven. The cookies should have expanded a bit, risen and begun to firm, but should still glisten a little bit and should not have cracked.

Remove from the oven and leave to cool for 5 minutes. Transfer them to a cooling rack and leave to cool for at least another 10–15 minutes.

MATCHA COOKIES WITH ALMONDS & WHITE CHOCOLATE

190g (6¾oz/¾ cup plus 1⅓ Tbsp) butter at
  refrigerator temperature, diced

135g (4¾oz/⅔ cup) light muscovado sugar

90g (3¼oz/scant ½ cup) caster (granulated) sugar

2 eggs

320g (11¼oz/scant 2½ cups) plain (all-purpose) flour

15g (½oz/2 Tbsp) cornflour (cornstarch)

10–15g (⅓–½oz/1–1½ Tbsp) high-quality matcha powder

5g (1⅔ tsp) baking powder

2g (⅔ tsp) salt

90g (3¼oz) white chocolate, roughly chopped

135g (4¾oz) + 50g (1¾oz) salted almonds,
  roughly chopped

ABOUT 15 COOKIES

These cookies were among the first to appear on my menu at Krümel. In my head, I had a pretty clear picture of a matcha cookie with white chocolate, since the bitterness of the matcha complements the sweetness and creaminess of white chocolate. To ensure a little texture and saltiness, I've also added large chunks of roasted salted almonds. Serve this cookie with a big cup of matcha latte – I promise you it's the perfect pairing!

Add the butter to your food processor or to the bowl of a stand mixer fitted with a paddle attachment and mix on a medium speed for 15 seconds until the butter begins to break up. Add both types of sugar and mix for about 30 seconds until everything is roughly mixed. Scrape the butter from the sides of the bowl.

Add the eggs and mix for 20 seconds until everything is just combined. Make sure you don't mix for too long – it's fine if it's still a little unmixed.

Combine the flour, cornflour, matcha powder, baking powder and salt in a separate bowl. Add the dry ingredients to the butter mixture in two batches, mixing for 15 seconds between each batch until everything is just combined. Scrape down the base and sides of the bowl between each round of mixing.

Finally, add the chocolate and the 135g (4¾oz) of roughly chopped almonds and mix at a low speed until they are roughly mixed into the dough.

Scoop 75g (2½oz) balls of dough using an ice cream scoop, or roll balls using 3 tablespoons of dough. There should be enough to make about 15 cookies. Sprinkle the 50g (1¾oz) of chopped almonds over the cookies and pat gently into the dough balls so that they stick. Place the dough balls in a container with a lid or on a tray that you then cover with cling film (plastic wrap). Leave to rest in the refrigerator for at least 3 hours – preferably overnight.

Preheat the oven to 190°C fan (210°C/ 410°F/gas 6–7).

Place the dough balls approximately 5cm (2in) apart on baking trays lined with baking parchment. Bake in the middle of the oven for 9–10 minutes. Bake one sheet at a time if not using a fan oven. The cookies should have expanded a bit, risen and begun to firm, but should still glisten a little bit and should not have cracked.

Leave the trays of cookies to cool for 5 minutes. Transfer them to a cooling rack and leave to cool for at least another 10–15 minutes.

S'MORES
COOKIES

190g (6¾oz/¾ cup plus 1⅓ Tbsp) butter at refrigerator temperature, diced
150g (5½oz/¾ cup) light muscovado sugar
90g (3¼oz/scant ½ cup) caster (granulated) sugar
2 eggs
320g (11¼oz/scant 2½ cups) plain (all-purpose) flour
10g (⅓oz/2 tsp) cornflour (cornstarch)
25g (1oz/¼ cup) cocoa powder
5g (1⅔ tsp) baking powder
3g (1 tsp) salt
180g (6¼oz) dark chocolate, roughly chopped
15 marshmallows

ABOUT 15 COOKIES

I first made these cookies at home with Hannah, a lovely Swedish-American girl, who wanted to help me out in the kitchen for two weeks. We convened in my kitchen on a daily basis to talk texture and flavour, and one day we got talking about how much fun it would be to make s'mores cookies. So we made our very own marshmallows with sesame seeds and small chunks of miso toffee. This recipe is simpler than that, and I think the dough with its dark cocoa is an even better match to the melted, toasted marshmallow.

The word s'mores comes from 'some more' and originated in the USA to describe an American treat consisting of toasted marshmallows and dark chocolate sandwiched between two graham crackers. You want 'some more' because it's so delicious! If you want to add a special finishing touch to your cookies, you can sprinkle some crumbled graham crackers or digestive biscuits across them after baking. Depending on how much time you have when baking, you can either make your own marshmallows or use shop-bought ones. For an extra melted, crispy finish, you can apply a little extra heat to your marshmallows using a kitchen blow torch after baking.

Add the butter to your food processor or to the bowl of a stand mixer fitted with a paddle attachment and mix on a medium speed for 15 seconds until the butter begins to break up. Add both types of sugar and mix for about 30 seconds until everything is roughly mixed. Scrape the butter from the sides of the bowl.

Add the eggs and mix for 20 seconds until everything is just combined. Make sure you don't mix for too long – it's fine if it's still a little unmixed.

Combine the flour, cornflour, cocoa, baking powder and salt in a separate bowl. Add the dry ingredients to the butter mixture in two batches, mixing for 15 seconds between each batch until everything is just combined. Scrape down the base and sides of the bowl between each round of mixing. Finally, add the chocolate and mix briefly at a low speed until the chocolate is roughly mixed into the dough.

Scoop 75g (2½oz) balls of dough using an ice cream scoop, or roll balls using 3 tablespoons of dough. There should be enough to make about 15 cookies. Press a marshmallow into the centre of each cookie and cover the edges of the marshmallow with a little dough. You want to make sure that it will be visible and bake nicely in the oven. Place the dough balls in a container with a lid or on a tray that you then cover with cling film (plastic wrap). Leave to rest in the refrigerator for at least 3 hours – preferably overnight.

→

Preheat the oven to 190°C fan (210°C/
410°F/gas 6–7).

Place the dough balls, marshmallow-side
up, approximately 5cm (2in) apart on baking
trays lined with baking parchment. Bake in
the middle of the oven for 9–10 minutes. Bake
one sheet at a time if not using a fan oven. The
cookies should have expanded a bit, risen and
begun to firm, but should still glisten a little bit
and should not have cracked.

Remove the trays from the oven and
leave to cool for 5 minutes. Transfer them
to a cooling rack and leave to cool for at
least another 10–15 minutes. If you have a
kitchen blow torch, finish off by toasting the
marshmallow until golden.

My top tip!
You'll only need to use the blow torch for a few seconds.

BLACK FOREST COOKIES

190g (6¾oz/¾ cup plus 1⅓ Tbsp) butter at refrigerator temperature, diced

150g (5½oz/¾ cup) light muscovado sugar

90g (3¼oz/scant ½ cup) caster (granulated) sugar

1½ tsp Kirsch (optional)

2 eggs

320g (11¼oz/scant 2½ cups) plain (all-purpose) flour

15g (½oz/2 Tbsp) cornflour (cornstarch)

25g (1oz/¼ cup) cocoa powder

5g (1⅔ tsp) baking powder

3g (1 tsp) salt

180g (6¼oz) dark chocolate, roughly chopped

90g (3¼oz) dried sour cherries

15 whole dark chocolate pellets

About 40g (1½oz) cacao nibs

ABOUT 15 COOKIES

I was born in Germany but quite some distance (380km) from the Schwarzwald – the Black Forest. I've only been there two or three times, but whenever I encounter a Black Forest gâteau on a menu or spot a dessert inspired by it, I get twinkly-eyed. This majestic, gooey cookie is inspired by the Black Forest gâteau, but skips the whipped cream you would customarily find in the layers on the cake. That said, feel free to serve the cookie with a dollop of lightly whipped cream – I promise you'll love it! I also like to add a little Kirsch to my dough – this spirit has a unique taste and the alcohol disappears during the bake (the cookie also works well without it).

Add the butter to your food processor or to the bowl of a stand mixer fitted with a paddle attachment and mix on a medium speed for 15 seconds until the butter begins to break up. Add both types of sugar and the Kirsch, if using, and mix for about 30 seconds until everything is roughly mixed. Scrape the butter from the sides of the bowl.

Add the eggs and mix for a maximum of 20 seconds until they are just combined. Make sure you don't mix for too long – it's fine if it's still a little unmixed.

Combine the flour, cornflour, cocoa, baking powder and salt in a separate bowl. Add the dry ingredients to the butter mixture in two batches, mixing for a maximum of 10–15 seconds between each batch until everything is just combined. Scrape down the base and sides of the bowl, between mixing.

Add the chopped chocolate and sour cherries and mix briefly at a low speed until they are roughly mixed into the dough.

Scoop 75g (2½oz) balls of dough using an ice cream scoop, or roll balls using 3 tablespoons of dough. There should be enough to make about 15 cookies. Press a chocolate pellet into each dough ball, then roll that side of the ball in the cacao nibs. Place the dough balls in a container with a lid or on a tray that you then cover with cling film (plastic wrap). Leave to rest in the refrigerator for at least 3 hours – preferably overnight.

Preheat the oven to 190°C fan (210°C/410°F/gas 6–7).

Place the dough balls, with the cacao nibs facing up, approximately 5cm (2in) apart on baking trays lined with baking parchment. Bake in the middle of the oven for 9–10 minutes. The cookies should have expanded a bit, risen and begun to firm, but should still glisten a little bit and should not have cracked.

Remove from the oven and leave to cool for 5 minutes. Transfer to a cooling rack and leave for at least another 10–15 minutes.

Black Forest cookies, page 70.

GOOEY
& SOFT

Dough balls rolled in sugar topping.

Just as the name suggests, these cookies are gooey and soft on the inside. They have a slightly airier and lighter crust than cookies made using cold or melted butter. The outside is lighter, smooth and glossy with crisp edges.

These kinds of cookies are made by beating butter and sugar until the batter takes on a lighter colour and becomes a little fluffier. The air beaten into them later serves as a raising agent together with the baking powder and bicarbonate of soda (baking soda) that are added. Be careful not to beat the ingredients too much or too little when making the recipes in this chapter.

There are many theories about how long to beat the sugar and butter. Some people go for a long time (5-7 minutes), working until the sugar crystals are no longer visible, the colour is pale and the consistency is very light and fluffy. Others beat the mixture for so little time that the sugar crystals crunch between your teeth as you eat these heavy cookies. Personally, I prefer the golden middle way...

I always aim for a slightly lighter coloured batter where the sugar crystals are only just visible. Start by whisking the butter for around 20 seconds. Then add the sugar and beat for 1½-2 minutes, pausing occasionally to scrape batter down from the sides of the bowl. Pay attention to exactly when it is time to stop whisking.

Use an ice cream scoop to make dough balls the right size.

Dough

The dough should be pliable, barely sticky and easy to shape into balls. The more you beat the butter and sugar, or the warmer your butter is, the stickier the dough will be. Spoon the dough into balls and roll them in the palms of your hands to give them a smooth surface before putting them in a plastic container and leaving them in the refrigerator for 3–24 hours. You can bake them right away if you're in a hurry, but the shape, texture, colour and flavour won't be as good as they would have been if the dough had been left to rest in the refrigerator.

Baking

When baking, the butter will slowly melt and the cookies will expand to about 7–8cm (3in) in diameter. Thanks to the aerated butter, baking powder and bicarbonate of soda, the cookies will rise in the oven and shouldn't then sink much at all when cooling. Gooey and soft cookies don't expand as much as those made using melted butter, and don't end up as thick as a chunky cookie.

Texture

The inside of the cookie will be gooey and very soft, and – if you've beaten the butter and sugar correctly – won't be too fluffy or cakey. The top will be smooth, with crispy, even edges and crumb that isn't too airy or gooey.

PEANUT BUTTER & CINNAMON COOKIES

140g (5oz/scant ⅔ cup) butter

40g (1½oz/2½ Tbsp) creamy peanut butter

120g (4¼oz/½ cup plus 1½ Tbsp) light muscovado sugar

70g (2½oz/5⅔ Tbsp) caster (granulated) sugar

1 egg

170g (6oz/1¼ cups) plain (all-purpose) flour

30g (1oz/3⅔ Tbsp) finely ground rye flour

1g (⅓ tsp) baking powder

3g (1 tsp) bicarbonate of soda (baking soda)

1½g (½ tsp) ground cinnamon

2g (⅔ tsp) salt

120g (4¼oz) roasted peanuts

80g (2¾oz) milk chocolate, roughly chopped

ABOUT 12 COOKIES

When baking cookies, you can generally replace regular dairy-based butter with any nut- or seed-based butter of your choosing. This very soft and creamy cookie uses both butter and peanut butter, in addition to whole peanuts for texture. The dough is also rolled in cinnamon sugar, which does wonders for the final product and further elevates that peanut flavour.

SUGAR TOPPING

40g (1½oz) caster (granulated) sugar

1 Tbsp ground cinnamon

Add the butter and peanut butter to your food processor or to the bowl of a stand mixer fitted with a paddle attachment and mix on a medium speed for 20 seconds until creamy. Add the sugars and mix for 1½–2 minutes until the sugar is well mixed into the butter. Scrape the butter from the sides of the bowl at 30-second intervals. The mixture should be light-coloured and with no visible crystals.

Add the egg and mix for 20 seconds until it is just combined. Make sure you don't mix for too long – it's fine if it's still a little unmixed.

Combine the plain flour, rye flour, baking powder, bicarbonate of soda, cinnamon and salt in a separate bowl. Add the dry ingredients to the butter mixture in two batches, mixing for 15 seconds between each batch until everything is just combined. Scrape down the base and sides of the bowl between each round of mixing.

Finally, add the peanuts and chocolate and mix quickly.

Scoop 65g (2¼oz) balls of dough using an ice cream scoop, or roll balls using 2 tablespoons of dough. There should be enough to make about 12 cookies. Roll the dough balls in the sugar topping and put them in a container with a lid or on a tray that you then cover with cling film (plastic wrap). Leave to rest in the refrigerator for at least 3 hours – preferably overnight.

Preheat the oven to 160°C fan (180°C/ 350°F/gas 4).

Place the dough balls approximately 5cm (2in) apart on baking trays lined with baking parchment. Bake in the middle of the oven for 12–13 minutes. The cookies should have expanded somewhat, risen and begun to develop a firm and glossy surface.

Remove the baking trays from the oven. Leave to cool for 5 minutes, then transfer them to a cooling rack and leave to cool for at least another 10–15 minutes.

Strawberry hibiscus cookies, page 82.

STRAWBERRY HIBISCUS COOKIES

150g (5½oz/⅔ cup) butter
finely grated zest of ½ lime
75g (2½oz/6 Tbsp) light muscovado sugar
120g (4¼oz/½ cup plus 1½ Tbsp) caster (granulated) sugar
1 egg
240g (8½oz/1¾ cups) plain (all-purpose) flour
3g (1 tsp) baking powder
3g (1 tsp) bicarbonate of soda (baking soda)
2g (⅔ tsp) salt
20g (⅔oz) + 30g (1oz) freeze-dried strawberry powder
15g (½oz) hibiscus powder

ABOUT 12 COOKIES

This recipe is inspired by Krümel's midsummer crumb that we only sell in the week leading up to Midsummer. This time around, I've added some dried hibiscus and lime zest to make the perfect summer cookie! It's easiest to find freeze-dried fruit online, in health-food stores and larger supermarkets. You can also use whole dried fruit that you run through your food processor first. By adding the fruit powder to the dough and sprinkling it over the baked cookies while they're still warm, you bring out the taste of strawberry in the best possible way.

Add the butter and lime zest to your food processor or to the bowl of a stand mixer fitted with a paddle attachment and mix on a medium speed for 20 seconds until the butter starts to become creamy. Add both types of sugar and mix for about 1½–2 minutes until the sugar is well mixed into the butter. Scrape the butter from the sides of the bowl at 30-second intervals. The mixture should be light in colour and with no visible crystals.

Add the egg and mix for 20 seconds until it is just combined. Make sure you don't mix for too long – it's fine if it's still a little unmixed.

Combine the flour, baking powder, bicarbonate of soda, salt, the 20g (⅔oz) of strawberry powder and the hibiscus powder in a separate bowl. Add the dry ingredients to the butter mixture in two batches, mixing for 15 seconds between each batch until everything is just combined. Scrape the base and sides of the bowl, between mixing.

Scoop 65g (2¼oz) balls of dough using an ice cream scoop, or roll balls using 2 tablespoons of dough. There should be enough to make about 12 cookies. Place the dough balls in a container with a lid or on a tray that you then cover with cling film (plastic wrap). Leave to rest in the refrigerator for at least 3 hours – preferably overnight.

Preheat the oven to 160°C fan (180°C/350°F/gas 4).

Place the dough balls approximately 5cm (2in) apart on baking trays lined with baking parchment. Bake in the middle of the oven for 11–12 minutes. Bake one sheet at a time if not using a fan oven. The cookies should have expanded a bit, risen and begun to develop a firm but slightly glistening surface.

Remove the baking trays from the oven and sprinkle the 30g (1oz) of strawberry powder over them. Leave to cool for 5 minutes, then transfer them to a cooling rack and leave to cool for at least another 10–15 minutes.

RASPBERRY COOKIES WITH ROSEWATER & WHITE CHOC

150g (5½oz/⅔ cup) butter

70g (2½oz/5⅔ Tbsp) light muscovado sugar

120g (4¼oz/½ cup plus 1½ Tbsp) caster
(granulated) sugar

1 egg

1½ Tbsp rosewater

235g (8½oz/1¾ cups) plain (all-purpose) flour

3g (1 tsp) baking powder

3g (1 tsp) bicarbonate of soda (baking soda)

2g (⅔ tsp) salt

20g (⅔oz) freeze-dried raspberry powder

130g (4½oz) white chocolate, roughly chopped

12 raspberries

ABOUT 12 COOKIES

Fresh raspberries bring a pleasant tartness to cookies and in this recipe they offset the sweetness of the white chocolate. As is common in Poland, I like to use rose petals, but if you want to ensure that the rose flavour is even throughout the bake then rosewater is better for this. Rosewater is a common ingredient in the Middle East and India – I love to add a few drops to fruit salads, panna cotta, cookie batter and madeleines, or use it together with raspberries, rhubarb and strawberries. If you want a little more texture to your cookies, adding 60–80g (2–3oz) pistachios to the dough works well.

Add the butter to your food processor or to the bowl of a stand mixer fitted with a paddle attachment and mix on a medium speed for 20 seconds until it is creamy. Add both types of sugar and mix for 1½–2 minutes until the sugar is well mixed into the butter. Scrape the butter down from the sides of the bowl at 30-second intervals. The goal is a fairly light-coloured mixture with no visible sugar crystals.

Add the eggs and rosewater and mix for 20 seconds until they are just combined. Make sure you don't mix for too long – it's fine if it's still a little unmixed.

Combine the flour, baking powder, bicarbonate of soda, salt and raspberry powder in a separate bowl. Add the dry ingredients to the butter mixture in two batches, mixing for 15 seconds between each batch until everything is just combined. Scrape the base and sides of the bowl, between mixing.

Finally, add the white chocolate and mix briefly at a low speed until the chocolate is roughly mixed into all the dough.

Scoop 65g (2¼oz) balls of dough using an ice cream scoop, or roll balls using 2 tablespoons of dough. There should be enough to make about 12 cookies. Press a raspberry into each dough ball. Place the dough balls in a container with a lid or on a tray that you then cover with cling film (plastic wrap). Leave to rest in the refrigerator for at least 3 hours – preferably overnight.

Preheat the oven to 160°C fan (180°C/350°F/gas 4).

Place the dough balls approximately 5cm (2in) apart on baking trays lined with baking parchment. Bake in the middle of the oven for 12–13 minutes. The cookies should have expanded, risen and begun to firm, but should still glisten a little bit and should not have cracked.

Remove the trays of cookies from the oven and leave to cool for 5 minutes. Transfer them to a cooling rack and leave to cool for at least another 10–15 minutes.

Use fresh rather than frozen berries for your topping – they are more acidic, taste better and look far more vibrant and delicious.

Dough balls topped with smashed fresh raspberries.

LEMON COOKIES WITH PISTACHIO & POPPY SEEDS

150g (5½oz/⅔ cup) butter

finely grated zest of ¾ lemon

75g (2½oz/6 Tbsp) light muscovado sugar

125g (4½oz/⅔ cup less 2 tsp) caster
   (granulated) sugar

1 egg

200g (7oz/1½ cups) plain (all-purpose) flour

40g (1½oz/3¼ Tbsp) finely ground rye flour

2g (⅔ tsp) baking powder

3g (1 tsp) bicarbonate of soda (baking soda)

2g (⅔ tsp) salt

130g (4½oz) + 24 pistachios, roasted

50g (1¾oz) poppy seeds, toasted

ABOUT 12 COOKIES

This cookie is for my friend Tati, who has been nagging me for a lemon cookie recipe for more than a year. When I started selling cookies, I did a selection box of five cookies, of which one happened to be lemon, miso and poppy seed. But after a few weeks I swapped it out, since I wasn't completely satisfied with the texture of the cookie. Then I went on to make a lemon and pistachio cookie with lavender that was only sold at Petit Marché, which is one of my favourite florists in Stockholm. And that was it for lemon cookies – until now.

Add the butter and lemon zest to your food processor or to the bowl of a stand mixer fitted with a paddle attachment and mix on a medium speed for 20 seconds until the butter starts to become creamy. Add both types of sugar and mix for 1½–2 minutes until the sugar is well mixed into the butter. Scrape the butter down from the sides of the bowl at 30-second intervals. The mixture should be fairly light in colour and with no visible sugar crystals.

Add the egg and mix for 20 seconds until it is just combined. Make sure you don't mix for too long – it's fine if it's still a little unmixed.

Combine the flour, rye flour, baking powder, bicarbonate of soda and salt in a separate bowl. Add the dry ingredients to the butter mixture in two batches, mixing for 15 seconds between each batch until everything is just combined. Scrape down the base and sides of the bowl between each round of mixing.

Add the 130g (4½oz) of roasted pistachios and mix quickly.

Scoop 65g (2¼oz) balls of dough using an ice cream scoop, or roll balls using 2 tablespoons of dough. There should be enough to make about 12 cookies. Press 2 pistachio nuts into each dough ball, then roll that side of the ball in the poppy seeds. Place the dough balls in a container with a lid or on a tray that you then cover with cling film (plastic wrap). Leave to rest in the refrigerator for at least 3 hours – preferably overnight.

Preheat the oven to 160°C fan (180°C/ 350°F/gas 4).

Place the dough balls approximately 5cm (2in) apart on baking trays lined with baking parchment. Bake in the middle of the oven for 11–12 minutes. Bake one sheet at a time if not using a fan oven. The cookies should have expanded a bit, risen and begun to develop a firm but slightly glistening surface.

Remove the trays of cookies from the oven and leave to cool for 5 minutes. Transfer them to a cooling rack and leave to cool for at least another 10–15 minutes.

MANGO, COCONUT & CHILLI COOKIES

150g (5½oz/⅔ cup) butter, at room temperature

70g (2½oz/5⅔ Tbsp) light muscovado sugar

130g (4½oz/⅔ cup) caster (granulated) sugar

1 egg

210g (7½oz/1½ cups) plain (all-purpose) flour

30g (1oz/3⅔ Tbsp) finely ground rye flour

3g (1 tsp) bicarbonate of soda (baking soda)

3g (1 tsp) baking powder

2g (⅔ tsp) salt

20g (⅔oz) freeze-dried mango powder

about 100g (3½oz) toasted coconut flakes

a few pinches of dried chilli (red pepper) flakes

ABOUT 12 COOKIES

This recipe was created on a hot day in June when I wanted to make a seasonal cookie that was refreshing and just a little bit tropical. Try as we might to work mainly with local ingredients, sometimes we make an exception for a really fun recipe. This cookie was a hit and left us longing for the return of those hot summer days once again. Don't forget to top them with a few chilli flakes, or if you can get hold of tajin seasoning, that's even better (it's often available from retailers stocking Mexican ingredients). A little heat makes a big difference!

Add the butter to your food processor or to the bowl of a stand mixer fitted with a paddle attachment and mix on a medium speed for 20 seconds until the butter starts to get creamy. Add both types of sugar and mix for 1½–2 minutes until the sugar is well mixed into the butter. Scrape the butter down from the sides of the bowl at 30-second intervals. The mixture should be fairly light in colour and with no visible sugar crystals.

Add the egg and mix for 20 seconds until it is just combined. Make sure you don't mix for too long – it's fine if it's still a little unmixed.

Combine the plain flour, rye flour, bicarbonate of soda, baking powder, salt and mango powder in a separate bowl. Add the dry ingredients to the butter mixture in two batches, mixing for 15 seconds between each batch until everything is just combined. Scrape down the base and sides of the bowl between each round of mixing.

Scoop 65g (2¼oz) balls of dough using an ice cream scoop, or roll balls using 2 tablespoons of dough. There should be enough to make about 12 cookies. Dip one side of the cookies into the coconut flakes and push down gently to ensure they stick. Place the dough balls in a container with a lid or on a tray that you then cover with cling film (plastic wrap). Leave to rest in the refrigerator for at least 3 hours – preferably overnight.

Preheat the oven to 160°C fan (180°C/350°F/gas 4).

Place the dough balls approximately 5cm (2in) apart on baking trays lined with baking parchment. Bake in the middle of the oven for 11–12 minutes. Bake one sheet at a time if not using a fan oven. The cookies should have expanded a bit, risen and begun to develop a firm but slightly glistening surface.

Remove the baking trays from the oven and sprinkle a few pinches of chilli flakes over the cookies. Leave to cool for 5 minutes, then transfer them to a cooling rack and leave to cool for at least another 10–15 minutes.

DOUBLE CHOCOLATE & LIQUORICE COOKIES

160g (5¾oz/¾ cup less 2 tsp) butter, at room temperature

100g (3½oz/½ cup) light muscovado sugar

70g (2½oz/5⅔ Tbsp) caster (granulated) sugar

1 egg

200g (7oz/1½ cups) plain (all-purpose) flour

20g (⅔oz/2⅓ Tbsp) finely ground rye flour

25g (1oz) unsweetened cocoa powder

3g (1 tsp) bicarbonate of soda (baking soda)

1g (⅓ tsp) baking powder

2g (⅔ tsp) salt

80g (2¾oz) dark chocolate (70% cocoa solids),
  roughly chopped

80g (2¾oz) dark milk chocolate (35–50% cocoa
  solids), roughly chopped

2–3 tsp liquorice root powder

about 2 tsp smoked sea salt or salt flakes

ABOUT 12 COOKIES

This is one of my favourite recipes from Krümel's first ever pop-up. It's full of surprises with a gentle hint of smoke offset by the sweet aniseed flavour of the liquorice root powder. Even people who claim not to like liquorice love this one! The cookie packs a mean punch with its two types of chocolate. It has a little acidity and bitterness thanks to the dark chocolate and unsweetened cocoa, while there is sweetness from the milk chocolate. It makes the perfect afternoon snack or after-dinner dessert.

Add the butter to your food processor or to the bowl of a stand mixer fitted with a paddle attachment and mix on a medium speed for 20 seconds until it is creamy. Add both types of sugar and mix for about 1½–2 minutes until the sugar is well mixed into the butter. Scrape the butter down from the sides of the bowl at 30-second intervals. The goal is a fairly light-coloured mixture with no visible sugar crystals.

Add the egg and mix for 20 seconds until it is just combined. Combine the flours, cocoa, bicarbonate of soda, baking powder and salt in a separate bowl. Add the dry ingredients to the butter mixture in two batches, mixing for 15 seconds between each batch until everything is just combined. Scrape down the base and sides of the bowl between each round of mixing.

Finally, add both types of chocolate and mix at a low speed until the chocolate is roughly mixed into all the dough.

Scoop 65g (2¼oz) balls of dough using an ice cream scoop, or roll balls using 2 tablespoons of dough. There should be enough to make about 12 cookies. Place the dough balls in a container with a lid. Leave to rest in the refrigerator for at least 3 hours – preferably overnight.

Preheat the oven to 160°C fan (180°C/ 350°F/gas 4).

Place the dough balls approximately 5cm (2in) apart on baking trays lined with baking parchment. Bake in the middle of the oven for 11–12 minutes. The cookies should have expanded, risen and begun to firm, but should still glisten a little bit – they may look a little underbaked.

Remove the trays from the oven and sprinkle the liquorice root powder and salt over the cookies. Leave to cool for 5 minutes, then transfer them to a cooling rack and leave to cool for at least another 10–15 minutes.

SAFFRON, PISTACHIO & WHITE CHOC COOKIES

150g (5½oz/⅔ cup) butter

½ tsp saffron threads or ¼ tsp saffron powder

115g (4oz/½ cup plus 1¼ Tbsp) caster

(granulated) sugar

80g (2¾oz/⅓ cup plus 1 Tbsp) light

muscovado sugar

1 egg

220g (7¾oz/1⅓ cups) plain (all-purpose) flour

30g (1oz/3⅔ Tbsp) spelt flour

3g (1 tsp) baking powder

3g (1 tsp) bicarbonate of soda

2g (⅔ tsp) salt

80g (2¾oz) roasted pistachios

100g (3½oz) caramelized white chocolate

(see page 96) or white chocolate chips,

roughly chopped

ABOUT 12 COOKIES

This is one of my favourite recipes! It's perfect for Christmas and should be a fixture in everyone's baking repertoire over the festive season. That's particularly true in a country like Sweden where everyone is obsessed with saffron – especially saffron buns – from November until Christmas Eve. Saffron and pistachio are without doubt one of the best combinations I know of. Adding caramelized white chocolate (or white chocolate chips) makes this cookie even more decadent and perfect for the holidays.

Add the butter to your food processor or to the bowl of a stand mixer fitted with a paddle attachment and mix on a medium speed for 20 seconds until the butter starts to get creamy.

Grind the saffron threads, if using, then mix with 1 tablespoon of the caster sugar. Add the saffron sugar, remaining caster sugar and muscovado to the butter. Mix for 1½–2 minutes until the sugar is well mixed into the butter. Scrape the butter from the sides of the bowl throughout. The mixture should be fairly light in colour and with no visible sugar crystals.

Add the egg and mix for 20 seconds until it is just combined. Make sure you don't mix for too long – it's fine if it's still a little unmixed.

Combine the flours, baking powder, bicarbonate of soda and salt in a separate bowl. Add the dry ingredients to the butter mixture in two batches, mixing for 15 seconds between batches until just combined. Scrape the base and sides of the bowl between mixing.

Add the pistachios and chocolate and mix briefly until they are relatively evenly distributed in the dough.

Scoop 65g (2¼oz) balls of dough using an ice cream scoop, or roll balls using 2 tablespoons of dough. There should be enough to make about 12 cookies. Place the dough balls in a container with a lid. Leave to rest in the refrigerator for at least 3 hours – preferably overnight.

Preheat the oven to 160°C fan (180°C/ 350°F/gas 4).

Place the dough balls approximately 5cm (2in) apart on baking trays lined with baking parchment. Bake in the middle of the oven for 12 minutes. The cookies should have expanded a bit, risen and begun to develop a firm but slightly glistening surface.

Remove from the oven and leave to cool for 5 minutes. Transfer to a cooling rack and leave to cool for at least 10–15 minutes.

Caramelized white chocolate

300g (10½oz) white chocolate (30%), roughly chopped

Caramelizing white chocolate takes a bit of work but it's definitely worth it. It becomes silkier, richer in texture and tastes like caramel. It's a little reminiscent of dulce de leche although a tad less sweet, and nuttier. Be careful during preparation as the chocolate gets very hot! You can cut up any leftovers and store in your refrigerator for up to 2 weeks.

Preheat the oven to 110°C fan (130°C/265°F/gas 1). Put the chocolate into an oven dish measuring approximately 20 x 20cm (8 x 8in) and put this in the middle of the oven.

Take the oven dish out every 10 minutes and stir the chocolate to make sure no pieces get stuck to the bottom or edges. Repeat this process 4–5 times until the chocolate begins to turn a dark beige colour and smells caramelized.

Mix the chocolate well with a spatula until it is creamy and runny. This may take a while, and to begin with the chocolate often feels a little hard.

Line a separate dish with cling film (plastic wrap) and pour the caramelized chocolate into it. Cover with cling film and leave to cool in the refrigerator. The chocolate should harden enough for you to be able to cut pieces from it to use in your cookie dough.

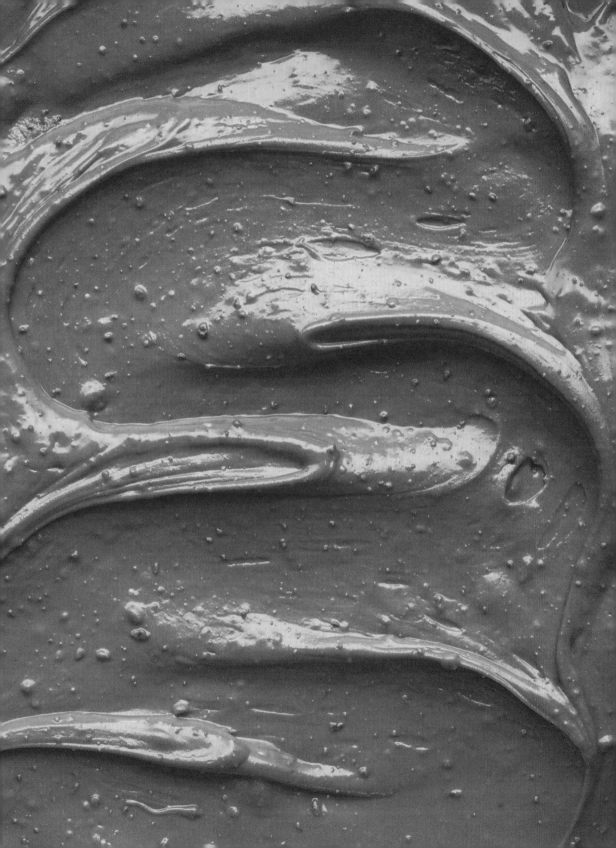

UBE BRÛLÉE COOKIES

150g (5½oz/⅔ cup) butter

80g (2¾oz/⅓ cup plus 1 Tbsp) light muscovado sugar

120g (4¼oz/½ cup plus 1½ Tbsp) caster (granulated) sugar, plus extra for burning

1 egg

½–¾ tsp liquid ube extract (purple sweet potato)

240g (8½oz/1¾ cups) plain (all-purpose) flour

3g (1 tsp) baking powder

3g (1 tsp) bicarbonate of soda (baking soda)

2g (⅔ tsp) salt

15g (½oz/1 Tbsp) ube powder (purple sweet potato powder)

70g (2½oz) white chocolate or caramelized white chocolate (see page 96), roughly chopped

ABOUT 12 COOKIES

This is a variation on the crème brûlée, Krümel's signature cookie, which features a brûléed top and vanilla cream filling. This cookie doesn't have a filling, but if you want to add one then you can, using a piping tube filled with something tasty like vanilla cream once you have finished baking. The ube is a purple sweet potato that originally hails from the Philippines and is used in desserts and baked goods. Apart from its beautiful purple colour, it also has a nutty taste rather like vanilla. It's available to buy as a concentrate in small bottles from Southeast Asian supermarkets, or alternatively in powdered form. I like to use both the extract and the powder for the perfect mixture of flavour and colour. After baking, sprinkle sugar over the cookies and burn it off just like you do with a crème brûlée.

Add the butter to your food processor or to the bowl of a stand mixer fitted with a paddle attachment and mix on a medium speed for 20 seconds until the butter starts to get creamy. Add both types of sugar and mix for 1½–2 minutes until the sugar is well mixed into the butter. Scrape the butter down from the sides of the bowl at 30-second intervals. The mixture should be fairly light in colour and with no visible sugar crystals.

Add the egg and ube extract and mix for 20 seconds until they are just combined. Make sure you don't mix for too long – it's fine if it's still a little unmixed.

Combine the flour, baking powder, bicarbonate of soda, salt and ube powder in a separate bowl. Add the dry ingredients to the butter mixture in two batches, mixing for 15 seconds between each batch until everything is just combined. Scrape the bowl, between mixing. Add the white chocolate and mix briefly.

Scoop 65g (2¼oz) balls of dough using an ice cream scoop, or roll balls using 2 tablespoons of dough. There should be enough to make about 12 cookies. Place the dough balls in a container with a lid or on a tray that you then cover with cling film (plastic wrap). Leave to rest in the refrigerator for at least 3 hours – preferably overnight.

Preheat the oven to 160°C fan (180°C/ 350°F/gas 4).

Place the dough balls approximately 5cm (2in) apart on baking trays lined with baking parchment. Bake in the middle of the oven for 11–12 minutes. Bake one sheet at a time if not using a fan oven. The cookies should have expanded a bit, risen and begun to develop a firm but slightly glistening surface and should not have cracked.

Remove the trays of cookies from the oven and leave to cool for 5 minutes. Transfer them to a cooling rack and leave to cool for at least another 10–15 minutes. Sprinkle a thin layer of sugar over the cookies and burn it using a kitchen blow torch. Allow to cool.

99

CHEWY & SOFT

Dough ball rolled in
sugar topping.

The recipes in this chapter are ideal for anyone who loves chewy, gooey and soft cookies.

In this case, we use melted butter instead of cold or soft butter. Melting butter means we skip beating the butter and sugar. Melted butter doesn't retain air in the same way, so just mix the sugar into the butter, followed by the eggs, using a hand whisk. Less air worked into the butter means less rise and slightly denser cookies.

Only by using melted butter can you achieve these really chewy and dense dough structures. There's almost no risk at all of your cookies ending up cakey. Another great thing about melted butter is that you can do everything by hand without the need for any machines.

Melting butter

Put the butter in a small saucepan and let it slowly melt on a low heat until almost all of it has melted. When there is only a small lump left, I usually take the saucepan off the hob to let it melt in the residual heat. Leave to cool for at least 15 minutes or until it reaches room temperature, then continue following the recipe. Butter that is too hot may melt the sugar, or even cook the eggs, which results in a disappointing texture.

Brown butter

I only use brown butter in two recipes in this book where I think it really makes a difference. One is paired with dark chocolate, with the brown butter giving a beautiful, nutty and caramelized flavour, while the other is with coffee, where the butter highlights the other flavours. As a general rule, I find that the taste of brown butter often gets drowned out in cookies and isn't as prominent as it is in other cookery.

Brown your butter by heating it in a small saucepan on a medium heat. Eventually, it will start to bubble and take on colour. Stir it occasionally using a wooden spoon. Pay attention to when it stops bubbling, and when the butter takes on a lovely amber colour and smells toasted and nutty you can take it off the hob. Take care to avoid burning it.

Dough

The melted butter makes the dough sticky and less dense. If you were to make balls using it and then bake them straight away, the cookies would end up very flat and chewy – give it a try if you're curious. Instead, I recommend that you leave the dough to cool in the refrigerator for between 45 minutes and 1 hour so that the dough sets. This will also make it easier to scoop balls from the dough. Roll the balls so that they have a smooth surface and leave them in the refrigerator for at least 3 hours. This makes a big difference and prevents the cookies from expanding too much.

Baking

Cookies with melted butter expand more than other cookies when baked, so don't worry when that happens. Right after you've taken them out of the oven they will be a little thick, but they will sink a little once they cool down.

Texture

The edges of these cookies will be uneven and crunchy. Their centres will be like fudge, and a little chewy. Would you prefer them to be thinner and chewier? Leave them in the refrigerator for less time when resting for the second time.

Brown butter chocolate chip cookies, page 104.

BROWN
BUTTER
CHOCOLATE
CHIP COOKIES

160g (5¾oz/¾ cup minus 2 tsp) butter,
browned (see page 103) and left to cool for
20–30 minutes

125g (4½oz/⅔ cup minus 2 tsp) light
muscovado sugar

70g (2½oz/5⅔ Tbsp) caster (granulated) sugar

10g (⅓oz/¾ Tbsp) dark sugar beet syrup
(or molasses)

1 egg

180g (6¼oz/1⅓ cups) plain (all-purpose) flour

20g (⅔oz/2⅓ Tbsp) spelt or emmer flour

3g (1 tsp) bicarbonate of soda (baking soda)

2g (⅔ tsp) baking powder

2g (⅔ tsp) salt

150g (5½oz) dark chocolate, roughly chopped

1 Tbsp sea salt flakes

ABOUT 12 COOKIES

My favourite cookie is – and always has been – the chocolate chip cookie. In the shop, we've come up with the perfect recipe for a super-gooey, rich and nutty cookie that many have declared to be 'the best cookie I have ever eaten'. For the book, I've adjusted the recipe a little, making it slightly chewier by using brown butter. I rarely use brown butter in cookies since I find the nutty flavour often gets drowned out by the other ingredients. However, there are exceptions to this, including this recipe. I love the brown butter with the dark chocolate, which really brings out the nuttiness of the spelt flour. This is a cookie with a beautiful uneven crust and crispy edges.

Beat the butter, muscovado sugar, caster sugar and syrup in a bowl using a balloon whisk for about 20 seconds.

Add the egg and beat until the batter is smooth.

Combine the plain flour, spelt flour, bicarbonate of soda, baking powder and salt in a separate bowl. Fold the dry ingredients into the butter mixture in two batches until they are just combined, ensuring that you scrape down the sides of the bowl between batches.

Finally, fold in the chocolate so that it is evenly distributed in the batter. Cover the bowl with a lid or cling film (plastic wrap) and leave to rest in the refrigerator for 45 minutes–1 hour.

Take out of the refrigerator and scoop 62g (2¼oz) balls of dough using an ice cream scoop, or roll balls using 2 tablespoons of dough. There should be enough to make about 12 cookies. For a more distinct flavour and taller cookies, place the dough balls in a container with a lid or on a tray that you then cover with cling film. Leave to rest in the refrigerator for at least 3 hours – preferably overnight.

Preheat the oven to 160°C fan (180°C/ 350°F/gas 4).

Place the dough balls approximately 5cm (2in) apart on baking trays lined with baking parchment. Bake in the middle of the oven for 11–12 minutes. Bake one sheet at a time if not using a fan oven. The cookies should have expanded, risen and begun to develop a firm but slightly glistening surface.

Remove the baking trays from the oven and sprinkle the cookies with sea salt. Leave to cool for 5 minutes, then transfer them to a cooling rack and leave to cool for at least another 10–15 minutes.

Brown butter chocolate chip
cookies with a small pinch of
sea salt, page 104.

CARDAMOM, COCONUT & COFFEE COOKIES

170g (6oz/¾ cup) butter, browned (see page 103) and left to cool for 20-30 minutes

130g (4½oz/⅔ cup) light muscovado sugar

70g (2½oz/5⅔ Tbsp) caster (granulated) sugar

1 egg

180g (6¼oz/1⅓ cups) plain (all-purpose) flour

20g (⅔oz/ 2⅓ Tbsp) spelt flour

3g (1 tsp) bicarbonate of soda (baking soda)

1g (⅓ tsp) baking powder

2g (⅔ tsp) salt

3g (1 tsp) freshly ground cardamom

5g (1 tsp) espresso instant coffee powder

5 Tbsp toasted coconut flakes

ABOUT 12 COOKIES

On my baker Kristina's first ever day working at Krümel, she said she would love it if we made a coconut coffee cookie. I'd previously made a cardamom and coffee cookie since the combo is just as good as a freshly baked cardamom bun and cup of freshly brewed coffee. Chucking some coconut into the mix sounded like an even better idea. Use coconut flakes instead of desiccated coconut – make sure you use bigger, wider pieces since they're tastier and provide more crunch.

Beat the brown butter, muscovado sugar and caster sugar in a bowl using a balloon whisk for about 20 seconds.

Add the egg and beat for about 30 seconds until the batter is smooth.

Combine the plain flour, spelt flour, bicarbonate of soda, baking powder, salt, cardamom and espresso instant coffee powder in a separate bowl. Fold the dry ingredients into the butter mixture in two batches until they are just combined, ensuring that you scrape down the sides of the bowl between batches.

Cover the bowl with a lid or cling film (plastic wrap) and leave to rest in the refrigerator for 1 hour.

Take out of the refrigerator and scoop 60g (2oz) balls of dough using an ice cream scoop, or roll balls using about 2 tablespoons of dough. There should be enough to make about 12 cookies. Roll the tops of the dough balls in the toasted coconut flakes. For a more distinct flavour and taller cookies, place the dough balls in a container with a lid or on a tray that you then cover with cling film. Leave to rest in the refrigerator for at least 3 hours – preferably overnight.

Preheat the oven to 160°C fan (180°C/ 350°F/gas 4).

Place the dough balls approximately 5cm (2in) apart on baking trays lined with baking parchment. Bake in the middle of the oven for 11–12 minutes. The cookies should have expanded, risen and begun to develop a firm but slightly glistening surface.

Remove the trays of cookies from the oven and leave to cool for 5 minutes. Transfer them to a cooling rack and leave to cool for at least another 10–15 minutes.

BLUEBERRY & LAVENDER COOKIES

160g (5¾oz/¾ cup minus 2 tsp) butter

1½ tsp dried lavender

120g (4¼oz/½ cup plus 1½ Tbsp) light muscovado sugar

75g (2½oz/6 Tbsp) + 1 Tbsp caster (granulated) sugar

1 egg

180g (6¼oz/1⅓ cups) plain (all-purpose) flour

30g (1oz/3⅔ Tbsp) finely ground rye flour

15g (½oz) + 30g (1oz) freeze-dried blueberry powder

1g (⅓ tsp) baking powder

3g (1 tsp) bicarbonate of soda (baking soda)

2g (⅔ tsp) salt

70–80g (2½–3oz) blueberries, washed

ABOUT 12 COOKIES

Blueberries always remind me of summers in Poland during my childhood. I spent parts of my childhood living in the country, and every other weekend we'd get into my grandparents' blue BMW to go to their summer place. Five minutes before we reached the tiny little wooden cottage, we'd always stop at the same lightly stocked rural general store. We bought *jagodzianki* (buns filled with blueberries) and I could hardly contain myself until I got to take my first bite. My grandmother used to make us a big pot of tea and then we would eat all the buns in the small forest clearing by their cottage. I wanted this cookie to evoke those memories alongside the feeling you get when you eat fresh blueberries. Best baked when blueberries are in season since that ensures the very best flavour – juicy and fruity. It's best to use wild blueberries since they are more flavourful and less watery and acidic than the ones grown in polytunnels.

Melt the butter in a small saucepan with the lavender. Leave to cool for 20–30 minutes, then sieve the butter and remove the flowers.

Beat the butter, muscovado sugar and the 75g (2½oz) of caster sugar in a bowl using a balloon whisk for about 20 seconds.

Add the egg and beat for about 30 seconds until the batter is smooth.

Combine the plain flour, rye flour, the 15g (½oz) blueberry powder, baking powder, bicarbonate of soda and salt in a separate bowl. Fold the dry ingredients into the butter mixture in two batches until they are just combined, ensuring that you scrape down the sides of the bowl between batches.

Mix the blueberries with the 1 tablespoon of caster sugar, then quickly fold the mixture into your batter. Cover the bowl with a lid or cling film (plastic wrap) and leave to rest in the refrigerator for 1 hour.

Take the dough out of the refrigerator and scoop 60g (2oz) balls of dough using an ice cream scoop, or roll balls using about 2 tablespoons of dough. There should be enough to make about 12 cookies. For a more distinct flavour and taller cookies, place the dough balls in a container with a lid or on a tray that you then cover with cling film. Leave to rest in the refrigerator for at least 3 hours – preferably overnight.

Preheat the oven to 160°C fan (180°C/350°F/gas 4).

Place the dough balls approximately 5cm (2in) apart on baking trays lined with baking parchment. Bake in the middle of the oven for 11–12 minutes. Bake one sheet at a time if not using a fan oven. The cookies should have expanded, risen and begun to develop a firm but slightly glistening surface.

Remove the trays of cookies from the oven and sprinkle the 30g (1oz) of blueberry powder over them. Leave to cool for 5 minutes, then transfer them to a cooling rack and leave to cool for at least another 10–15 minutes.

TOMATO
& VANILLA
COOKIES

160g (5¾oz/¾ cup minus 2 tsp) butter, melted
and left to cool for 20–30 minutes

100g (3½oz/½ cup) light muscovado sugar

60g (2oz/5 Tbsp) caster (granulated) sugar

10g (⅓oz/¾ Tbsp) dark sugar beet syrup

3g (1 tsp) vanilla powder or 2½ tsp vanilla extract

1 egg

160g (5¾oz/scant 1¼ cups) plain
(all-purpose) flour

20g (⅔oz/2⅓ Tbsp) finely ground rye flour

30g (1oz) dried tomato powder

1g (⅓ tsp) baking powder

2g (⅔ tsp) bicarbonate of soda (baking soda)

1g (⅓ tsp) salt

ABOUT 12 COOKIES

I'm obsessed with tomatoes, so it's no surprise that when they're in season in August and September my kitchen is full to bursting with them. I use them in salads, add them to oil, ferment them, roast them in the oven or just eat them fresh. This cookie took people by surprise in the early days, but it's gone on to become a bestseller in the shop. It tastes sweet, acidic and a little fruity – not to mention the fact that it's chewy, gooey and brings molasses to mind. Although the nigella seeds make a big difference, you can definitely skip them or swap them out for lightly toasted sesame seeds, if you prefer.

SUGAR TOPPING

2 tsp nigella seeds (black onion seeds)
or toasted sesame seeds

40g (1½oz/3¼ Tbsp) caster (granulated) sugar

Beat the butter, muscovado sugar, caster sugar, syrup and vanilla in a bowl using a balloon whisk for about 30 seconds.

Add the egg and beat until the batter is smooth.

Mix the plain flour, rye flour, tomato powder, baking powder, bicarbonate of soda and salt in a separate bowl. Fold the dry ingredients into the butter mixture in two batches until they are just combined, ensuring that you scrape down the sides of the bowl between batches.

Cover the bowl with a lid or cling film (plastic wrap) and leave to rest in the refrigerator for 1 hour.

Take out of the refrigerator and scoop 62g (2¼oz) balls of dough using an ice cream scoop, or roll balls using about 2 tablespoons of dough. There should be enough to make about 12 cookies.

Mix the nigella seeds with the sugar and roll one side of each dough ball in the sugar topping. For a more distinct flavour and taller cookies, place the dough balls in a container with a lid or on a tray that you then cover with cling film. Leave to rest in the refrigerator for at least 3 hours – preferably overnight.

Preheat the oven to 160°C fan (180°C/350°F/gas 4).

Place the dough balls approximately 5cm (2in) apart on baking trays lined with baking parchment. Bake in the middle of the oven for 11–12 minutes. Bake one sheet at a time if not using a fan oven. The cookies should have expanded, risen and begun to develop a firm but slightly glistening surface.

Remove the trays of cookies from the oven and leave to cool for 5 minutes. Transfer them to a cooling rack and leave to cool for at least another 10–15 minutes.

SPICE &
PECAN
COOKIES

160g (5¾oz/¾ cup minus 2 tsp) butter, melted and left to cool for 20–30 minutes

120g (4¼oz/½ cup plus 1½ Tbsp) light muscovado sugar

70g (2½oz/5⅔ Tbsp) caster (granulated) sugar

3 Tbsp maple syrup

1 egg

220g (7¾oz/1⅔ cups) plain (all-purpose) flour

1g (⅓ tsp) baking powder

3g (1 tsp) bicarbonate of soda (baking soda)

1½ tsp pumpkin spice (see right)

2g (⅔ tsp) salt

150g (5½oz) pecans, roasted and roughly chopped

SUGAR TOPPING

1–2 tsp pumpkin spice (see right)

40g (1½oz/3¼ Tbsp) caster (granulated) sugar

ABOUT 12 COOKIES

Contrary to what the name might suggest, pumpkin spice contains no pumpkin but is actually a spice mix used in the USA when making pumpkin pie. This spice mix has spread far beyond its home borders and is now used in other baking, coffees and desserts. It's a festive mix containing cinnamon, allspice, ginger and nutmeg. Use a pre-mixed pumpkin spice or make your own following the recipe below. This is the perfect cookie to eat in the autumn as the leaves begin to turn and you need a sweet treat to bring you some comfort and warmth.

PUMPKIN SPICE

10g (1½ Tbsp) ground cinnamon

3g (1 tsp) ground ginger

2g (⅔ tsp) ground nutmeg

2g (⅔ tsp) ground dried garlic

1g (¼ tsp) ground allspice

⅛ tsp freshly ground black pepper

Mix all the spices for the pumpkin spice in a small bowl and set to one side.

Beat the butter, muscovado sugar, caster sugar and maple syrup in a bowl using a balloon whisk for about 30 seconds. Add the egg and beat until the batter is smooth.

Mix the flour, baking powder, bicarbonate of soda, pumpkin spice and salt in a separate bowl. Fold the dry ingredients into the butter mixture in two batches until they are just combined, ensuring that you scrape down the sides of the bowl between batches. Finally, fold in the pecans, ensuring they are evenly distributed in the dough. Cover the bowl with a lid and leave to rest in the refrigerator for 1 hour.

Take out of the refrigerator and scoop 62g (2¼oz) balls of dough using an ice cream scoop, or roll balls using about 2 tablespoons of dough. There should be enough to make about 12 cookies.

Mix together the ingredients for the sugar topping and roll one side of each dough ball in it (see overleaf).

For a more distinct flavour and taller cookies, place the dough balls in a container with a lid or on a tray that you then cover with cling film. Leave to rest in the refrigerator for at least 3 hours – preferably overnight.

Preheat the oven to 160°C fan (180°C/ 350°F/gas 4).

Place the dough balls approximately 5cm (2in) apart on baking trays lined with baking parchment. Bake in the middle of the oven for 11–12 minutes. The cookies should have expanded, risen and begun to develop a firm but slightly glistening surface.

Remove the trays of cookies from the oven and leave to cool for 5 minutes. Transfer them to a cooling rack and leave to cool for at least another 10–15 minutes.

Press one side of the dough ball into the sugar topping.

Divide the dough and roll into balls. Mix the ingredients for the sugar topping well. Carefully take each dough ball and press it gently into the sugar topping. Cover at least half the ball with sugar.

GARAM MASALA & RAISIN COOKIES

118

1 chai or Earl Grey tea bag, or equivalent volume of tea leaves

150ml (5fl oz/scant ⅔ cup) boiling water

130g (4¾oz/scant 1 cup) raisins or 120g (4¼oz/scant 1 cup) sultanas (golden raisins)

160g (5¾oz/¾ cup minus 2 tsp) butter, melted and left to cool for 20–30 minutes

120g (4¼oz/½ cup plus 1½ Tbsp) light muscovado sugar

70g (2½oz/5⅔ Tbsp) caster (granulated) sugar

1 egg

200g (7oz/1½ cups) plain (all-purpose) flour

1g (⅓ tsp) baking powder

3g (1 tsp) bicarbonate of soda (baking soda)

2g (⅔ tsp) salt

1 tsp garam masala

ABOUT 12 COOKIES

Garam masala is an Indian spice mix more frequently used in dishes like chicken tikka masala and chana masala than in desserts. However, it's a spice mix that is the perfect complement to raisins, bananas, ginger and apple. I soak my raisins in chai, but you could also use Earl Grey or another flavoured tea – or even rum or another good-quality spirit. I find this slightly chewy cookie really addictive!

SUGAR TOPPING

1½ tsp garam masala

40g (1½oz/3¼ Tbsp) caster (granulated) sugar

Put the tea bag in the boiling water and leave it to stew for 5 minutes. Remove the tea bag and add the raisins and leave to stand for 10 minutes. Drain the water and carefully dry the raisins without piercing them, then set to one side.

Beat the butter and both sugars in a bowl using a balloon whisk for about 30 seconds.

Add the egg and beat for about 30 seconds until the batter is smooth.

Mix the flour, baking powder, bicarbonate of soda, salt and garam masala in a separate bowl. Fold the dry ingredients into the butter mixture in two batches until they are just combined, ensuring that you scrape down the sides of the bowl between batches. Carefully fold in the raisins.

Cover the bowl with a lid and leave to rest in the refrigerator for 1 hour. Then, scoop 62g (2¼oz) balls of dough using an ice cream scoop, or roll balls using about 2 tablespoons of dough. There should be enough to make about 12 cookies.

Mix together the garam masala and sugar for the topping and roll the tops of the dough balls in the spiced sugar.

For a more distinct flavour and taller cookies, place the dough balls in a container with a lid or on a tray that you then cover with cling film. Leave to rest in the refrigerator for at least 3 hours – preferably overnight.

Preheat the oven to 160°C fan (180°C/350°F/gas 4).

Place the dough balls approximately 5cm (2in) apart on baking trays lined with baking parchment. Bake in the middle of the oven for 12–13 minutes. Bake one sheet at a time if not using a fan oven. The cookies should have expanded, risen and begun to develop a firm but slightly glistening surface.

Remove the trays of cookies from the oven and leave to cool for 5 minutes. Transfer them to a cooling rack and leave to cool for at least another 10–15 minutes.

LEBKUCHEN TOFFEE COOKIES

160g (5¾oz/¾ cup minus 2 tsp) butter

110g (3¾oz/½ cup plus 1 Tbsp) light
  muscovado sugar

70g (2½oz/5⅔ Tbsp) caster (granulated) sugar

Finely grated zest of ½ tangerine

1 egg

180g (6¼oz/1⅓ cups) plain (all-purpose) flour

20g (⅔oz/2⅓ Tbsp) spelt flour

1g (⅓ tsp) baking powder

3g (1 tsp) bicarbonate of soda (baking soda)

1½g (½ tsp) salt

4g (1½ tsp) gingerbread spice mix, see right

110g (3¾oz) toffee, finely chopped

ABOUT 12 COOKIES

Lebkuchen is the German word for gingerbread. It comes in all sorts of shapes, sizes and consistencies. Variations of this spice mix can be found in many countries. What all the varieties have in common is that they contain gingerbread spices (or *Lebkuchengewürz*). The spice mix featured here works well in other cookies and biscuits and is particularly good with slightly spicy, full-bodied and earthy tones.

GINGERBREAD SPICE MIX

35g (6 Tbsp) ground cinnamon

6g (2 tsp) ground cloves

1½g (½ tsp) ground ginger

¼ tsp ground nutmeg

1½g (½ tsp) ground cardamom

3g (1 tsp) ground star anise

3g (1 tsp) ground allspice

Combine all the ingredients for the gingerbread spice mix in a separate bowl and set to one side.

Melt the butter in a small saucepan. Leave to cool for 20–30 minutes.

Beat the butter and sugars in a bowl using a balloon whisk for about 30 seconds. Add the tangerine zest, then add the egg and beat until smooth.

Combine the flours, baking powder, bicarbonate of soda, salt and the 1½ teaspoons of spice mix in a separate bowl. Fold the dry ingredients into the butter mixture in two batches until they are just combined, ensuring that you scrape the sides of the bowl between batches.

Mix the toffee into the dough, then cover the bowl with a lid and leave to rest in the refrigerator for 1 hour.

Take out of the refrigerator and scoop 62g (2¼oz) balls of dough using an ice cream scoop, or roll balls using about 2 tablespoons of

dough. There should be enough to make about 12 cookies.

For a more distinct flavour and taller cookies, place the dough balls in a container with a lid or on a tray that you then cover with cling film. Leave to rest in the refrigerator for at least 3 hours – preferably overnight.

Preheat the oven to 160°C fan (180°C/ 350°F/gas 4).

Place the dough balls approximately 5cm (2in) apart on baking trays lined with baking parchment. Bake in the middle of the oven for 11–12 minutes. Bake one sheet at a time if not using a fan oven. The cookies should have expanded, risen and begun to develop a firm but slightly glistening surface.

Remove the trays of cookies from the oven and leave to cool for 5 minutes. Transfer them to a cooling rack and leave to cool for at least another 10–15 minutes.

Once the sugar and butter have been mixed together, add your zest. I love the smell of citrus!

Fill the ice cream scoop right up to the rim. If you want to be precise with your dough balls, then weigh them out.

Before making the dough balls, finish by stirring in the pieces of toffee.

VEGAN & GLUTEN-FREE

Gluten-free hazelnut
and Earl Grey
cookies as dough
balls and fully
baked cookies.

Gluten-free and vegan cookies are super-tasty. It's just a case of knowing how to replace wheat flour, eggs and sugar while not losing any flavour or texture along the way. In our shop we always have a number of popular vegan options on rotation. Sometimes one of our seasonal specials will also happen to be vegan or gluten-free. It turns out that you can bake incredible cookies with a little help from oats and buckwheat, and that eggs and butter are replaceable. Many of my favourite cookies are now vegan.

Vegan cookies

For me, it's essential that a vegan cookie still feels deliciously decadent. I've tried a number of butter alternatives, including regular margarine, plant-based margarines, cold-pressed coconut oil, and Naturli vegan block. All of these work just fine as butter replacements, but my favourite is vegan block. It contains the fewest additives and is made from shea butter, coconut oil, rapeseed (canola) oil and carrot juice. Unlike margarine, vegan block goes pretty hard when left in the refrigerator and doesn't soften as quickly when you put it into your food processor or stand mixer. The melting point for shea butter is 28–32°C (82–90°F), which is pretty close to the melting point for regular butter, which is about 28–36°C (82–97°F). Coconut oil melts at 23°C (73°F). The combination of fats in the vegan block means that it melts at the right speed in the oven without expanding too much. However, it is very important that the cookies go straight from the refrigerator to the oven when it's time to bake them, and you must always leave them to cool for a few minutes. Vegan block is usually available in most major supermarkets. If you're working with an alternative vegan margarine, then you may need to add 10–20g (⅓–⅔oz) coconut oil to your dough to help it along.

There are a number of ways to replace eggs – including flax seed, apple sauce and bananas. My preferred method is to use oat milk: replacing one egg with 55–57ml (2fl oz) oat milk (which is what I do in the two eggless recipes in this book) makes for the perfect cookie.

Dough

Vegan dough ends up being very similar to the chunky dough described in this book. Make sure that the vegan butter really is refrigerator temperature when you add it, so there are a few lumps of the butter left in the dough. By not mixing together the fat and sugar, you help to make sure that it melts more slowly.

The liquid in the form of vegan milk is added in the penultimate step – this means that before mixing in the milk, the dough is dry and crumbly, a bit like a regular scone dough. After you add the oat milk, keep mixing until the milk is just incorporated, but no longer as this will result in gluten forming in the dough. Work quickly and make sure your dough balls are uneven and chunky.

Baking

The bake time is shorter and the oven temperature higher so that they expand less while gaining a crunchy outside and a super gooey middle. Since they don't contain any eggs, there's no need to worry about them not being in the oven for long enough.

Texture

The Hazelnut & Tahini and the Chunky Double Choc will give you thick, chunky cookies that are soft and gooey on the inside but with a crunchy surface and edges. I think they taste best when they've had 30 minutes to cool and the chocolate is still a little melted.

Gluten-free cookies

There are lots of options if you want to avoid regular wheat flour when baking – these include oat flour, buckwheat flour, nut flours, coconut flour and many others. All of them result in a distinctive character and flavour profile, which means some are better suited to cookies than others.

If you replace wheat flour with gluten-free flour, then you will need to use less flour or increase the volume of liquid (milk, butter, eggs) – otherwise your dough will end up dry and crumbly. You may also need to slightly increase the amount of baking powder to get the right texture.

Dough

Buckwheat and oat flour both absorb a lot of water, which will mean the doughs seem stickier and wetter than the other recipes in this book. For this reason, it's a good idea to rest them in the refrigerator for 30–60 minutes after mixing, before then scooping the dough balls and leave them in the refrigerator for at least 3 hours and preferably overnight.

Baking

Gluten-free cookies should be baked for 10–12 minutes at 160°C fan (180°C/350°F/ gas 4). They will expand slowly and bake evenly on the inside while remaining deliciously gooey.

Texture

The two gluten-free recipes in this book have very different textures. The first is crumbly due to the oat flour, while the second has a thin and crispy surface with a chewier inside due to the meringue technique.

As a rule, you can expect gluten-free cookies to be crumblier than other kinds, but I think it varies from recipe to recipe based on the ratio of ingredients. It's quite possible to bake the perfect cookie without wheat flour.

VEGAN MILKY HAZELNUT & TAHINI COOKIES

150g (5½oz/⅔ cup) refrigerator-cold vegan butter (vegan block or margarine), diced

50g (1¾oz/3½ Tbsp) tahini paste

15g (½oz/1 Tbsp) coconut oil

130g (4½oz/⅔ cup) light muscovado sugar

100g (3½oz/½ cup) caster (granulated) sugar

320g (11¼oz/2½ cups minus 1 Tbsp) plain (all-purpose) flour

30g (1oz/3⅔ Tbsp) spelt flour

20g (⅔oz/3 Tbsp) cornflour (cornstarch)

5g (1⅔ tsp) baking powder

2g (⅔ tsp) salt

65ml (2¼fl oz/4½ Tbsp) plant-based milk

160g (5¾oz) vegan milk chocolate, roughly chopped

100g (3½oz/¾ cup) hazelnuts, roasted

ABOUT 15 COOKIES

Tahini, milk chocolate and hazelnuts are such a great match! Tahini makes this cookie dough very silky and creamy, but the chunks of hazelnut and chocolate provide a bit of bite. While some may miss butter in vegan cookies, you barely notice its absence in this one made using a vegan butter. Make sure to let the dough rest for long enough in the refrigerator that the vegan butter has time to harden before you roll the dough balls.

Add the vegan butter, tahini and coconut oil to your food processor or to the bowl of a stand mixer fitted with a paddle attachment and mix on a medium speed for 15 seconds until the butter begins to break up. Add both types of sugar and mix for about 30 seconds until everything is roughly mixed. Scrape the butter down from the sides of the bowl.

Combine the flours, baking powder and salt in a separate bowl. Add the dry ingredients to the butter mixture in two batches, mixing for 15 seconds between each batch until everything is just combined. Scrape down the base and sides of the bowl between each round of mixing.

Add the milk and mix the dough until smooth and even.

Finally, add the chocolate and hazelnuts and mix at a low speed until it is roughly mixed into the dough.

Scoop 75g (2½oz) balls of dough using an ice cream scoop, or roll balls using 3 tablespoons of dough. There should be enough to make about 15 cookies. Place the dough balls in a container with a lid or on a tray that you then cover with cling film (plastic wrap). Leave to rest in the refrigerator for at least 3 hours – preferably overnight.

Preheat the oven to 190°C fan (210°C/410°F/gas 6–7).

Place the dough balls approximately 5cm (2in) apart on baking trays lined with baking parchment. Bake in the middle of the oven for 9–10 minutes until the cookies are done. Bake one sheet at a time if not using a fan oven. The cookies should have expanded a bit, risen and begun to firm, but should still glisten a little bit and should not have cracked.

Remove the baking trays from the oven. Leave the cookies to cool for 5 minutes on the tray, then transfer them to a cooling rack and leave to cool for at least another 10–15 minutes.

VEGAN CHUNKY DOUBLE CHOC COOKIES

190g (6¾oz/¾ cup plus 1 tsp) refrigerator-cold vegan butter (vegan block or margarine), diced
130g (4½oz/⅔ cup) light muscovado sugar
100g (3½oz/½ cup) caster (granulated) sugar
320g (11¼oz/1½ cups minus 1½ Tbsp) plain (all-purpose) flour
30g (1oz/⅓ cup) cocoa powder
20g (⅔oz/3 Tbsp) cornflour (cornstarch)
5g (1⅔ tsp) baking powder
3g (1 tsp) salt
70ml (2¼fl oz/4½ Tbsp) plant-based milk
130g (4¾oz) vegan milk chocolate, roughly chopped
70g (2½oz) vegan dark chocolate, roughly chopped

ABOUT 15 COOKIES

This is a decadent, majestic cookie with a texture reminiscent of the Black Forest and s'mores cookies – the one difference being that it is 100 per cent vegan. It features very simple flavouring with just chocolate and cocoa. It's best eaten while still a little warm and at its most gooey.

Add the butter to your food processor or to the bowl of a stand mixer fitted with a paddle attachment and mix on a medium speed for 15 seconds until the butter begins to break up. Add both types of sugar and mix for about 30 seconds until everything is roughly mixed. Scrape the butter down from the sides of the bowl.

Combine the flour, cocoa, cornflour, baking powder and salt in a separate bowl. Add the dry ingredients to the butter mixture in two batches, mixing for 15 seconds between each batch until everything is just combined. Scrape down the base and sides of the bowl between each round of mixing. Add the milk and mix the dough until smooth.

Finally, add both types of chocolate and mix at a low speed until they are roughly mixed into the dough.

Scoop 75g (2½oz) balls of dough using an ice cream scoop, or roll balls using 3 tablespoons of dough. There should be enough to make about 15 cookies. Place the dough balls in a container with a lid or on a tray that you then cover with cling film (plastic wrap). Leave to rest in the refrigerator for at least 3 hours – preferably overnight.

Preheat the oven to 190°C fan (210°C/410°F/gas 6–7).

Place the dough balls approximately 5cm (2in) apart on baking trays lined with baking parchment. Bake in the middle of the oven for 9–10 minutes until the cookies are done. Bake one sheet at a time if not using a fan oven. The cookies should have expanded a bit, risen and begun to firm, but should still glisten a little bit and should not have cracked.

Remove the baking trays from the oven. Leave the cookies to cool for 5 minutes on the tray, then transfer them to a cooling rack and leave to cool for at least another 10–15 minutes.

TRIPLE CHOC & OAT GLUTEN-FREE COOKIES

165g (5¾oz/¾ cup minus 1 tsp) butter

90g (3¼oz/scant ½ cup) light muscovado sugar

70g (2½oz/5⅔ Tbsp) caster (granulated) sugar

1 egg

240g (8½oz/2½ cups) oat flour

3g (1 tsp) baking powder

3g (1 tsp) bicarbonate of soda

2g (⅔ tsp) salt

30g (1oz) white chocolate, roughly chopped

70g (2½oz) milk chocolate, roughly chopped

50g (1¾oz) dark chocolate, roughly chopped

ABOUT 12 COOKIES

Oat flour is a great alternative to regular wheat flour and gives this cookie a toasty, sweet flavour. It tastes like a decadent bowl of porridge stuffed to the brim with chocolate. It's up to you what ratio of chocolate types you include up to the total weight. The finished cookie has a very soft texture, although it remains almost a little crumbly.

Add the butter to your food processor or to the bowl of a kitchen stand mixer fitted with a paddle attachment and mix on a medium speed for 15 seconds until the butter begins to break up. Add both types of sugar and mix for about 1½–2 minutes until everything is roughly mixed. Scrape the butter down from the sides of the bowl. The mixture should be slightly lighter in colour and with no visible sugar crystals.

Add the egg and beat for about 20 seconds until it is just mixed. Make sure you don't mix for too long – it's fine if there are still small flecks of egg visible.

Combine the oat flour, baking powder, bicarbonate of soda and salt in a separate bowl. Add the dry ingredients to the butter mixture in two batches, mixing for 15 seconds between each batch until everything is just combined. Scrape down the base and sides of the bowl between each round of mixing.

Fold all the chopped chocolate into the dough.

Scoop 65g (2¼oz) balls of dough using an ice cream scoop, or roll balls using 2 tablespoons of dough. There should be enough to make about 12 cookies. Place the dough balls in a container with a lid or on a tray that you then cover with cling film (plastic wrap). Leave to rest in the refrigerator for at least 3 hours – preferably overnight.

Preheat the oven to 160°C fan (180°C/ 350°F/gas 4).

Place the dough balls approximately 5cm (2in) apart on baking trays lined with baking parchment. Bake in the middle of the oven for 12 minutes until the cookies are done. Bake one sheet at a time if not using a fan oven. The cookies should have expanded a bit, risen and begun to firm, but should still glisten a little bit and should not have cracked.

Remove the baking trays from the oven. Leave the cookies to cool for 5 minutes on the tray, then transfer them to a cooling rack and leave to cool for at least another 10–15 minutes.

HAZELNUT &
EARL GREY
GLUTEN-FREE
COOKIES

136

1 egg

90g (3¼oz/scant ½ cup) light muscovado sugar

70g (2½oz/5⅔ Tbsp) caster (granulated) sugar

160g (5¾oz/¾ cup less 2 tsp) butter, melted and left to cool for 10 minutes

200g (7oz/heaped 1½ cups) buckwheat flour

3g (1 tsp) baking powder

2g (⅔ tsp) salt

3g (1 tsp) Earl Grey tea leaves, crushed

80g (2¾oz/¾ cup) roasted hazelnuts, roughly chopped

120g (4¼oz) dark chocolate, roughly chopped

ABOUT 12 COOKIES

Buckwheat flour isn't new – it's been around for a long time in Asia and Europe, where it's used in products such as noodles, bread and pancakes. I was raised on buckwheat – mostly as a side to salty meals – and I must confess that I didn't fall head over heels for it. That's all changed, and nowadays I want to add buckwheat to most things – there's nothing like roasted buckwheat in cookies and other sweet baked treats. It gives a beautiful nuttiness. I don't usually bake with just buckwheat since it has a pretty intense taste, but when combined with an aromatic Earl Grey, roasted hazelnuts and dark chocolate it really does hit the spot.

Add the egg to your food processor or to the bowl of a stand mixer fitted with a balloon whisk attachment and mix on a medium speed for 10 seconds. Add both types of sugar and mix for 6 minutes until well-mixed and fluffy, as when making meringues. Stir in the melted and cooled butter.

Combine the buckwheat flour, baking powder, salt and Earl Grey tea leaves in a separate bowl. Add the dry ingredients to the butter mixture by hand in two batches, mixing until everything is just combined.

Fold in the chopped hazelnuts and chocolate, then cover the bowl with a lid or cling film (plastic wrap) and leave to rest in the refrigerator for 1 hour.

Scoop 65g (2¼oz) balls of dough using an ice cream scoop, or roll balls using 2 tablespoons of dough. There should be enough to make about 12 cookies. Place the dough balls in a container with a lid or on a tray that you then cover with cling film. Leave to rest in the refrigerator for at least 3 hours – preferably overnight.

Preheat the oven to 160°C fan (180°C/ 350°F/gas 4).

Place the dough balls approximately 5cm (2in) apart on baking trays lined with baking parchment. Bake in the middle of the oven for 11–12 minutes until the cookies are done. Bake one sheet at a time if not using a fan oven. The cookies should have expanded somewhat, risen and begun to develop a firm surface. They should look quite dry on the outside but shouldn't be very cracked.

Remove the baking trays from the oven. Leave the cookies to cool for 5 minutes on the tray, then transfer them to a cooling rack and leave to cool for at least another 10–15 minutes.

LEFT-OVER COOKIES

When making krüm'balls, start by dipping the balls in melted chocolate, then roll them in chopped hazelnuts.

We all know that the probability of there being a few cookies left over is pretty unlikely. But in the event that it does happen, this is the solution.

Twelve to fifteen cookies (the standard batch for recipes in this book) sometimes ends up being a little too much. They keep for 3–5 days and you can always freeze them, defrost them and warm them up another time. But if you forget to do this and just happen to have a few cookies lying around your kitchen for a few days, then they are the perfect ingredients for one of the recipes in this section of the book.

Crumble the cookies and store in a jar. Use them to top your yogurt, fruit salad or ice cream.

Make a bread pudding with cookie crumbs instead of dry bread.

You can also make a pie crust using old cookies.

Have you ever made your own cookie butter? Mix 200g (7oz) cookies, 40g (1½oz/3 Tbsp butter), 10g (⅓oz/2½ tsp) light muscovado sugar, 2g (¾ tsp) sea salt flakes, 1 Tbsp honey and 30–40ml (2–2½ Tbsp) condensed milk in a food processor until smooth. All done! You can also use this to fill the cookies on page 52.

KRÜM'BALLS

8–10 leftover cookies

2–5 Tbsp dairy or plant-based milk

1 shot of espresso (about 25ml/1fl oz)

100g (3½oz) milk chocolate

1 Tbsp rapeseed (canola) oil

200g (7oz/2 cups) hazelnuts, crushed in a
food processor

MAKES 10–15

I always try to avoid food waste, both in the shop and at home. At the shop, we bake all our cookies on the day and try to predict as best we can how many we're going to sell. Even so, we sometimes sell out or have a few cookies left over at closing time. Taking inspiration from Sweden's chocolate balls and their 'Punsch rolls' (infused with liqueur, covered in marzipan and dipped in dark chocolate), I made this recipe using mashed up old cookies mixed with milk and espresso before rolling them in chocolate and nuts. It's delicious! Krüm'balls go soft and chewy at room temperature, and harder and fudgier when kept in the refrigerator – both work for me! They keep for about three weeks in the freezer and one week in the refrigerator. Feel free to add spices like cinnamon, cardamom and vanilla according to taste.

Crumble the cookies into as small pieces as possible and put them in a food processor or into the bowl of a stand mixer fitted with a paddle attachment. Blitz for about 1 minute until the crumbs are even smaller.

Add 2 tablespoons of the milk and the espresso and mix until it begins to resemble a dough. The dough should be pliable and not too dry or too sticky. Add more milk if it seems too hard.

Roll the dough into balls of about 35–40g (1¼–1½oz) and put them in a container with a lid or on a tray that you then cover with cling film (plastic wrap). Leave to rest in the refrigerator for about 1 hour.

Put the chocolate and rapeseed oil into a heatproof bowl and melt over a saucepan quarter-filled with simmering water. Put the crushed hazelnuts in a separate bowl.

Take the balls out of the refrigerator. Dip one side of each ball into the melted chocolate before rolling it in your hands until it's covered in chocolate. It's much easier if you wear plastic gloves to do this! Roll the balls in the hazelnuts until they are covered all over.

Put the balls in a container with a lid and leave in the refrigerator for 20–30 minutes until they are set and ready to be eaten.

It's easier to dip the balls into the melted chocolate
if you wear plastic gloves.

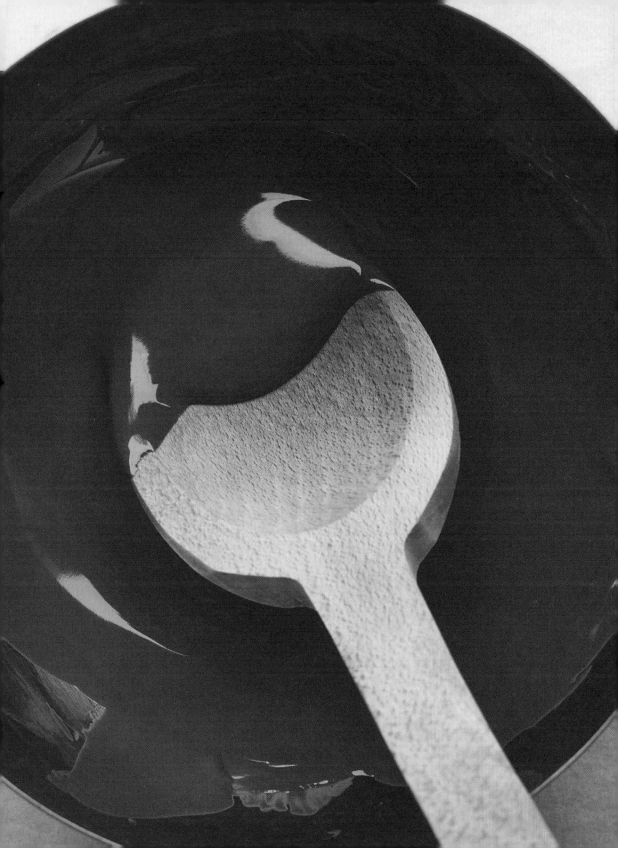

COOKIE
SANDWICHES

About 4 leftover cookies (2 rounds per cookie, depending on size)

4 Tbsp dulce de leche

Desiccated (dried shredded) coconut, for rolling (optional)

MAKES 4

I lived in Argentina's capital, Buenos Aires, for three months. I moved there to learn Spanish, but I mostly ended up falling for the food. Apart from discovering my passion for *sándwiches de miga* (with the crusts cut off), I also fell in love with dulce de leche. This is a kind of caramel cream made with condensed milk and found across Argentina. You can easily make dulce de leche by making a small hole in a tin of condensed milk and then boiling it for 2 hours in a saucepan filled with water and covered with a lid. It's also just fine to buy ready-made dulce de leche.

Dulce de leche is also used to make *alfajores* – a dulce de leche-filled sandwich made of two crumbly cookies and sometimes rolled in coconut flakes. This is my version of *alfajores*. Don't use cookies that are more than three days old, as you want the sandwich to be soft.

Cut out eight rounds from your leftover cookies using a round pastry cutter (a small glass also works well), about 2–3cm (¾–1¼in) in diameter.

Add 1 tablespoon of dulce de leche to four of the rounds and place the remaining rounds on top of these to form four small sandwiches. Serve immediately or keep in the refrigerator for up to 3 days.

If you like, you can also roll the sides in desiccated coconut.

KRÜMELISU

300g (10½oz) fresh strawberries, diced

2 Tbsp caster (granulated) sugar

1 tsp sumac

70ml (2¼fl oz/4½ Tbsp) whole milk

2–4 leftover cookies, depending on size

SERVES 4

This multi-layered dessert is a little reminiscent of the mighty tiramisu, but instead of coffee and amaretto the cookies are soaked in milk.

It's the perfect dessert for dinner with friends. Don't make the recipe more than 6 hours in advance to ensure that the cream remains fluffy. Sumac is available from Middle Eastern specialist retailers and larger supermarkets. Sumac goes beautifully with strawberries and gives the dessert a delicate acidity and striking crimson colour.

CREAM

200g (7oz/¾ cup plus 2 Tbsp) mascarpone cheese

1 tsp rosewater

1 tsp vanilla extract

250g (9oz/generous 1 cup) whipping cream

50g (1¾oz/¼ cup) caster (granulated) sugar

Mix the strawberries, caster sugar and sumac in a bowl and leave to stand for 20 minutes at room temperature.

To make the cream, thoroughly mix the mascarpone, rosewater and vanilla together. Whisk the cream with the sugar until the mixture is fluffy and holds its shape without being too stiff, then fold this into the mascarpone mixture.

Spoon 4 tablespoons of the cream mixture into four glasses or bowls.

Pour the milk into a small bowl. Dip 1–2 cookies into the milk, then crumble over the cream in the glasses. Cover each glass with 2 tablespoons of the strawberries.

Repeat the process for the second layer of cream, cookies and strawberries. If there is any strawberry juice left in the bowl, spoon this over the top of the four desserts.

Leave to cool in the refrigerator for at least 30 minutes before serving.

RECIPE INDEX

Matcha cookies with almonds & white chocolate, page 64

ACKNOWLEDGEMENTS

I want to express my heartfelt gratitude to my loving and very patient boyfriend Johan, who has always believed in me and supported me. Thank you to my mum and dad, who have always believed in me no matter what I have done and who have encouraged me to follow my own path.

Thanks also to my sister and her boyfriend for all their honest feedback during recipe testing and for pushing me to keep improving.

Thanks to the whole gang at the Krümel shop in Stockholm for making it such a great place to work and for all the help they offer on a daily basis.

Special thanks to Maria Nilsson for getting in touch and guiding me along the way – writing this book has been a dream come true. Thanks to Lennart Weibull and Sara Edström for making this book more beautiful than I could have imagined.

Thanks to all my friends who have bravely sampled different flavours and eaten far too many cookies.

Finally, my thanks go to everyone who has supported me and my cookie business, and to all my customers who keep eating my cookies – without you there wouldn't be a book.

Kaja Hengstenberg is the owner of Krümel, a small cookie shop in Stockholm. She has worked as a recipe developer and private chef, ran supper clubs, pop-up events and cookery classes and over the years has contributed to numerous publications. The inspiration for opening her own cookie store came from living in London, New York and Paris. She is based in Stockholm, Sweden.

Cookies & Crumbs first published by Natur & Kultur, Sweden

This English language hardback edition published in 2024
by Quadrille, an imprint of Hardie Grant Publishing
52–54 Southwark Street
London SE1 1UN
quadrille.com

For the original Swedish edition:
Photographer Lennart Weibull
Retouching Linnea Herner
Layout Sara Edström
Editor & translation of recipes Maria Nilsson
Translation of all other texts Henrik Francke

For the English language hardback edition:
Managing Director Sarah Lavelle
Commissioning Editor Stacey Cleworth
Translation from Swedish Ian Giles
Designers Gemma Hayden, Emily Lapworth
Head of Production Stephen Lang
Senior Production Controller Sabeena Atchia

Cataloguing in Publication Data: a catalogue record for this book
is available from the British Library.

Text © Kaja Hengstenberg 2023
Layout © Quadrille 2024

ISBN 9781837831449
Printed in China

FSC
www.fsc.org

MIX
Paper | Supporting
responsible forestry
FSC™ C020056